# Artistic Impressions by Bob Routh

Cats and Kittens
Coloring book for Grownups
Original Art by
Artistic Impressions by Bob Routh
DOGS and PUPS
Original Art by
Artistic Impressions by Bob Routh
Available NOW !!
on Amazon
New Books coming
out each week!
Keep watching!!!

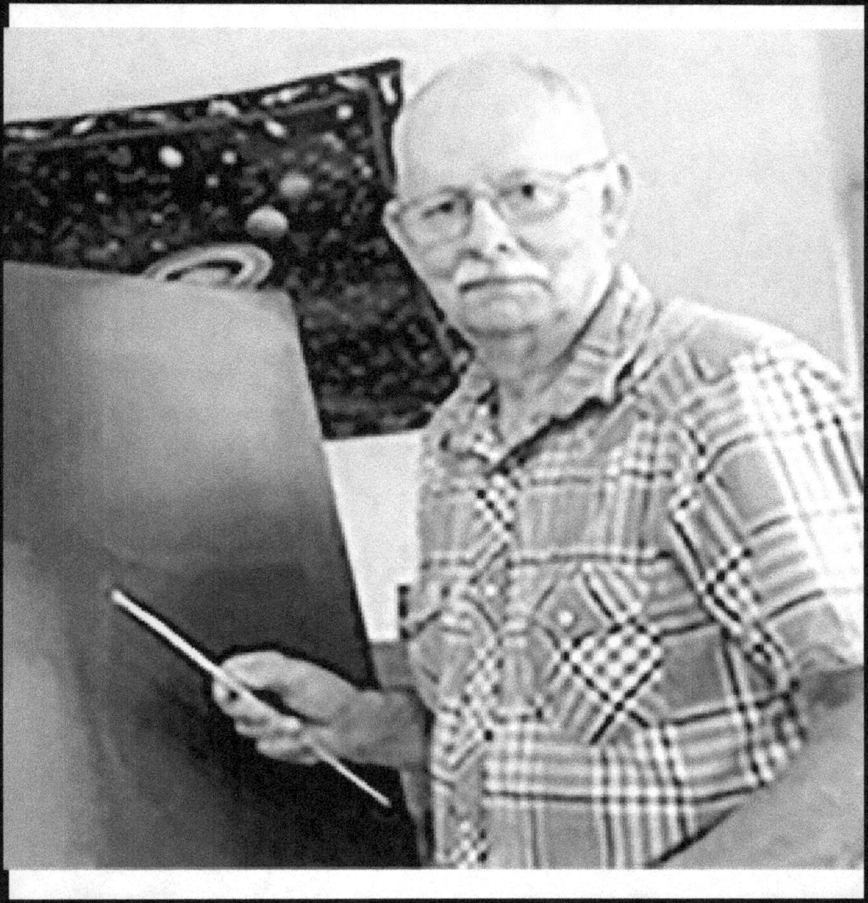

Artistic Impressions by
Bob Routh


https://www.facebook.com/ArtisticImpressionsByBob

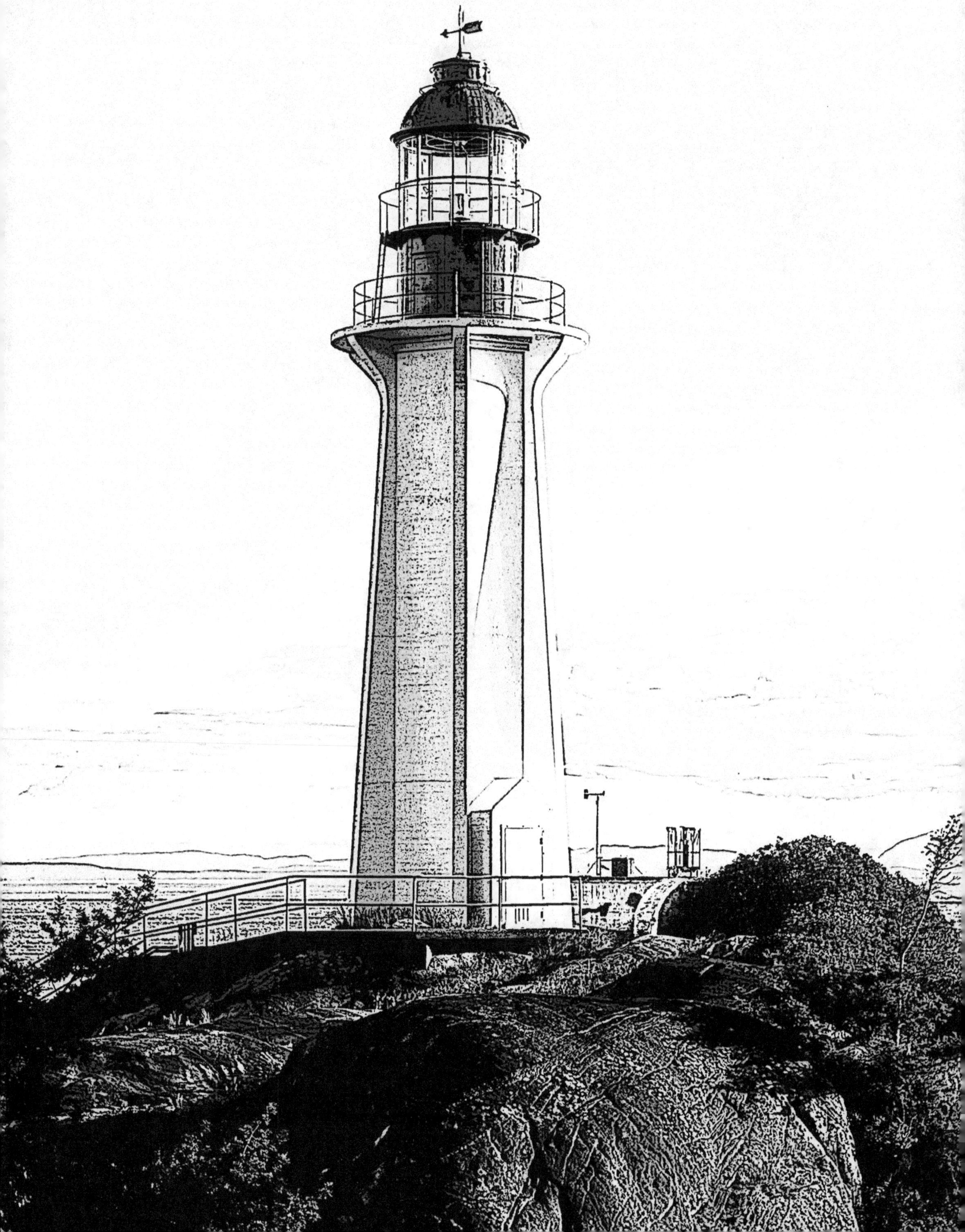

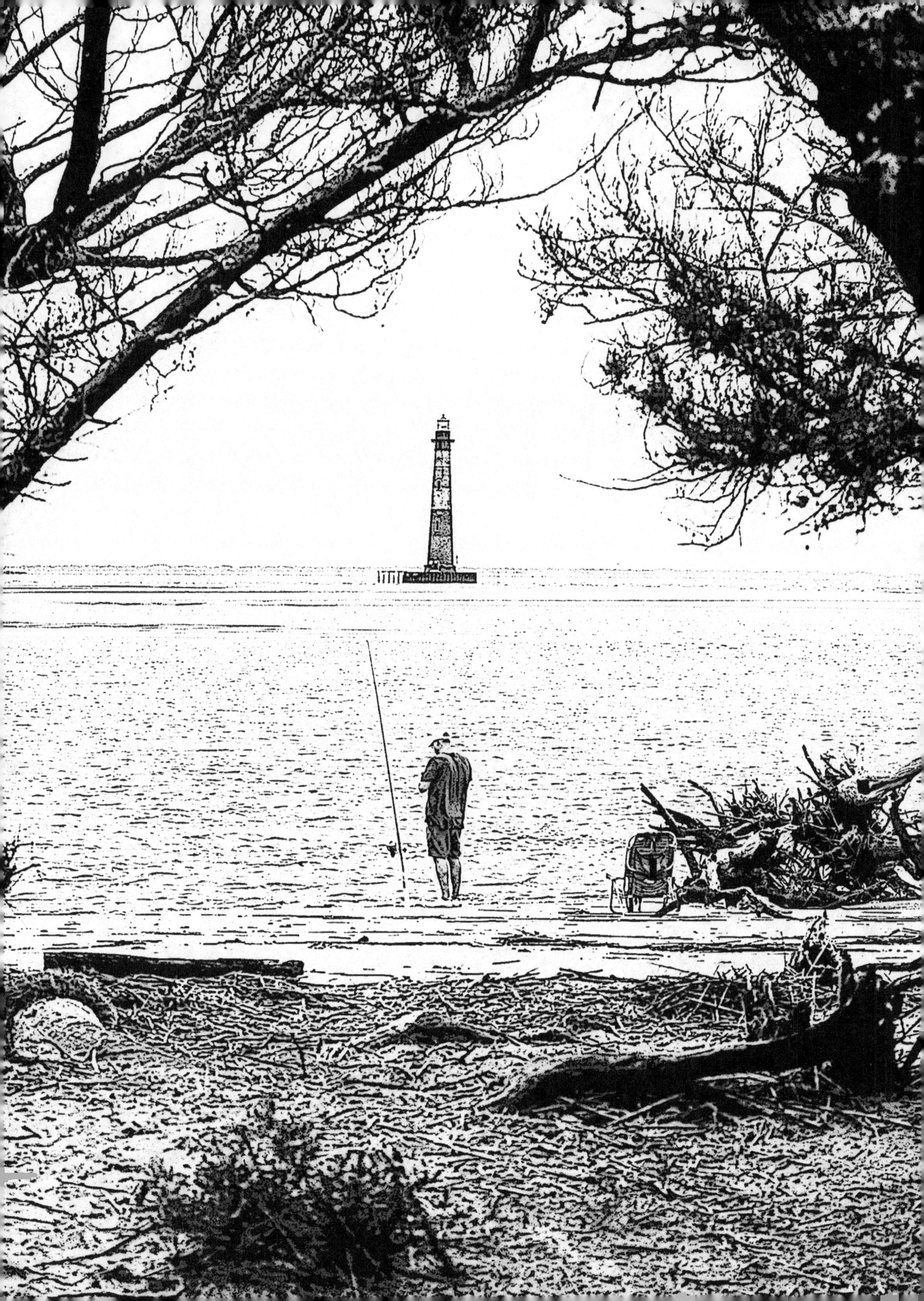

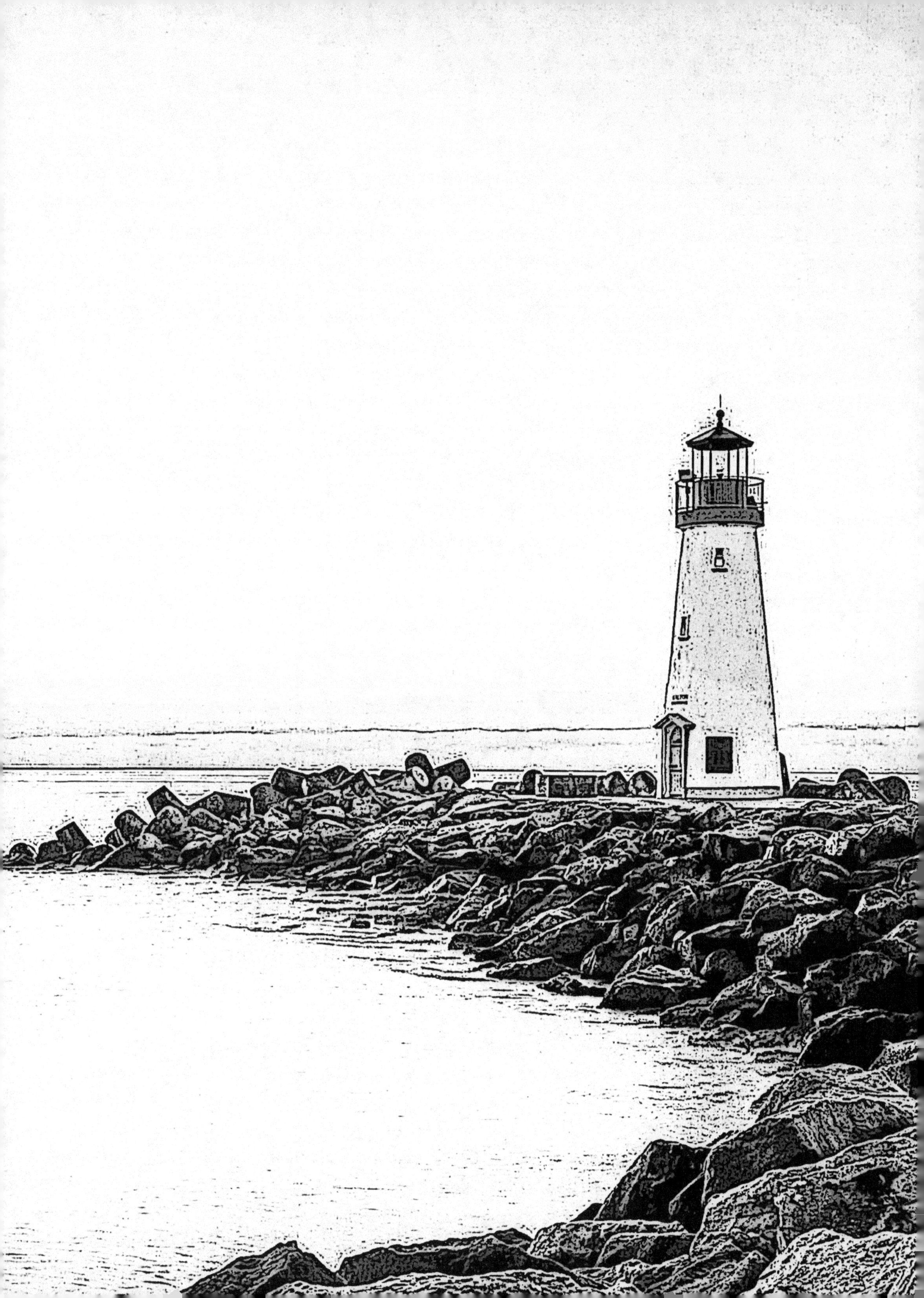

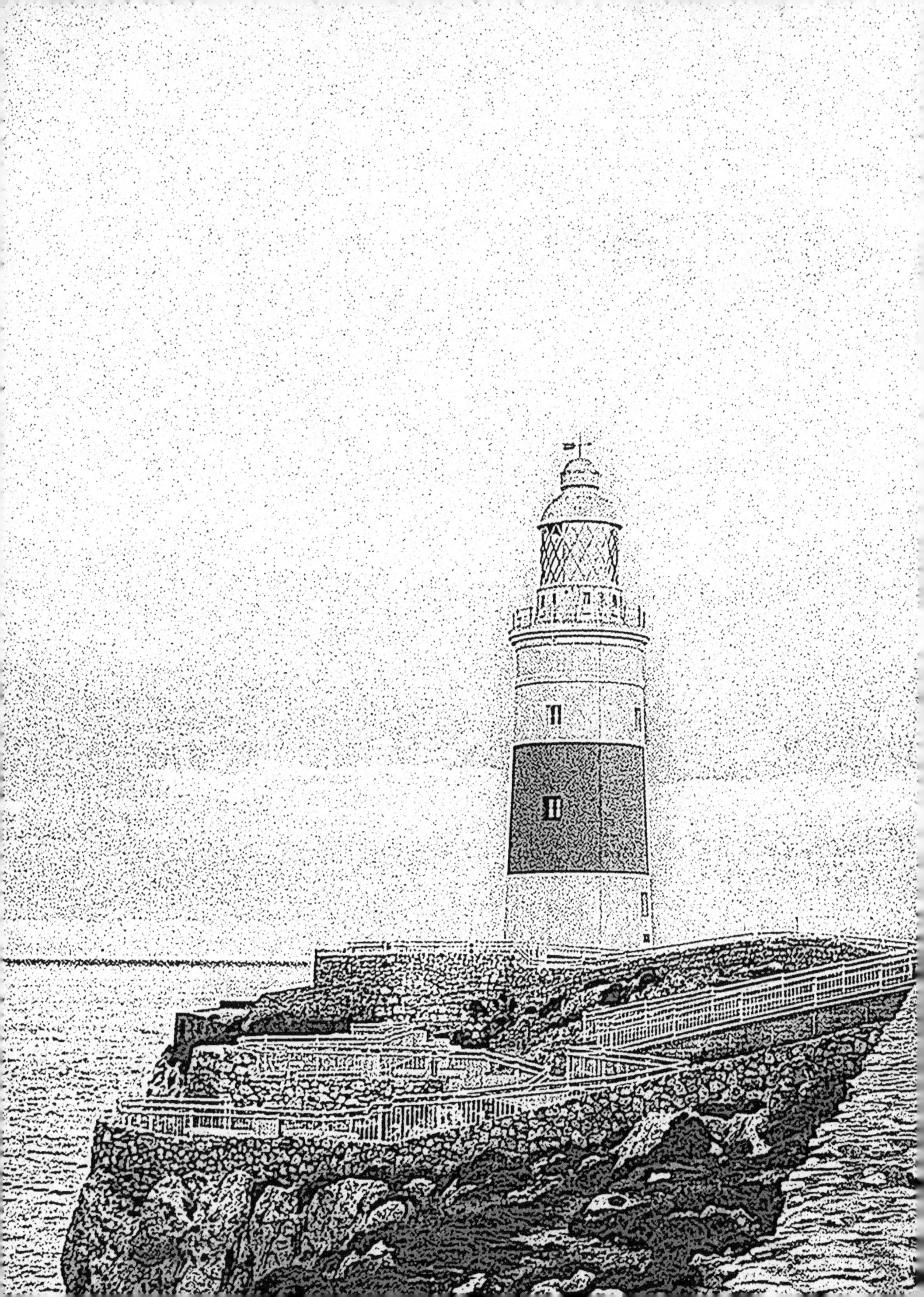

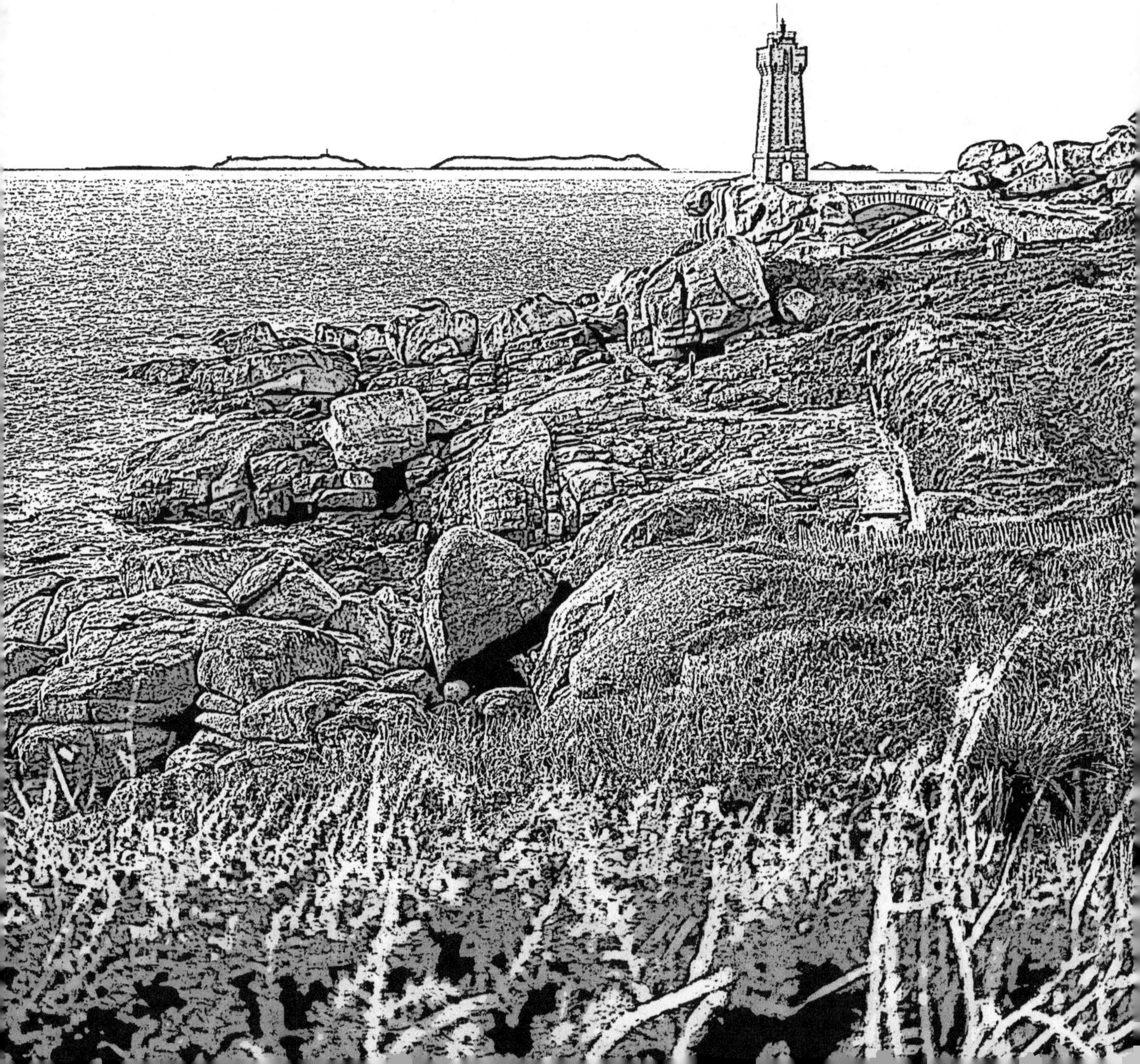

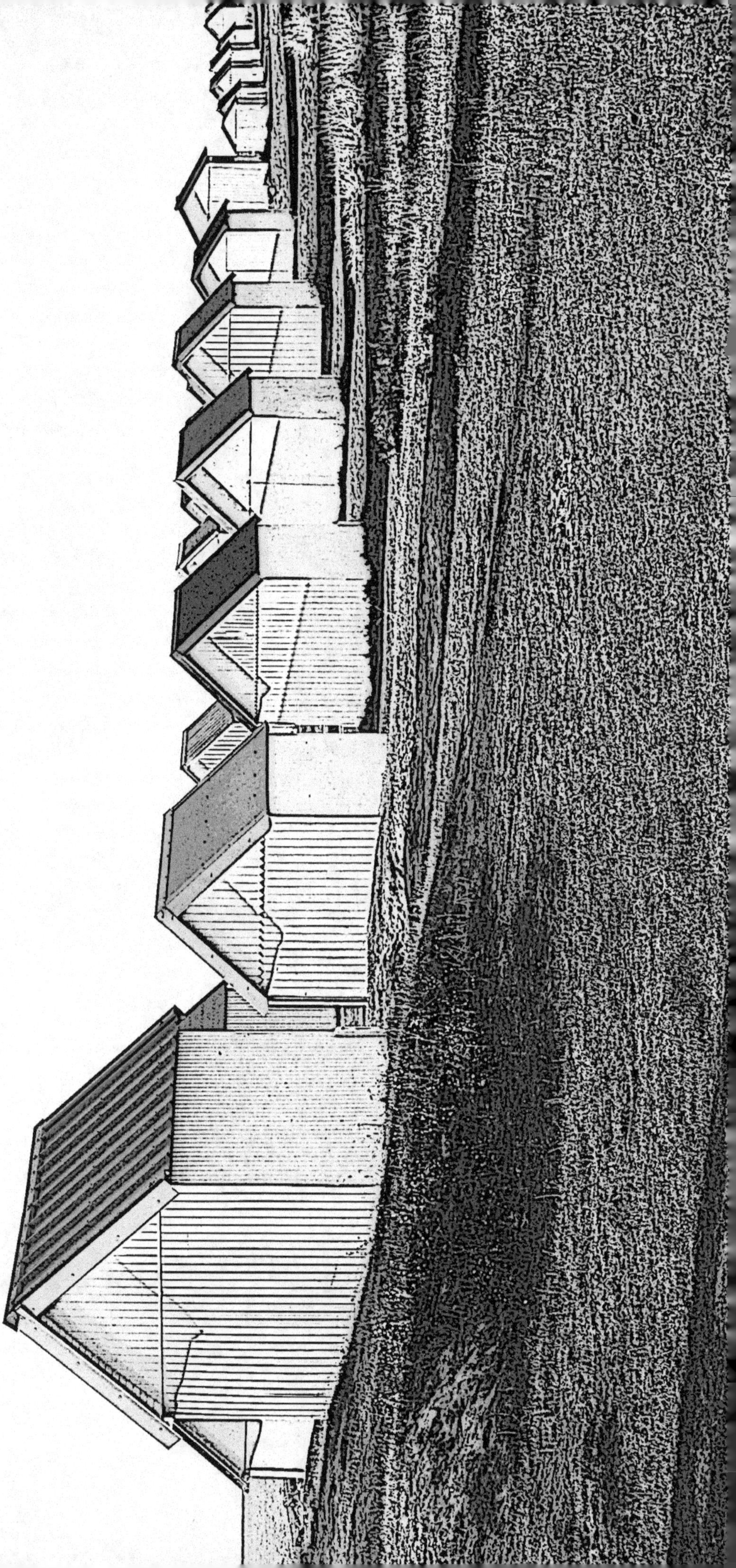

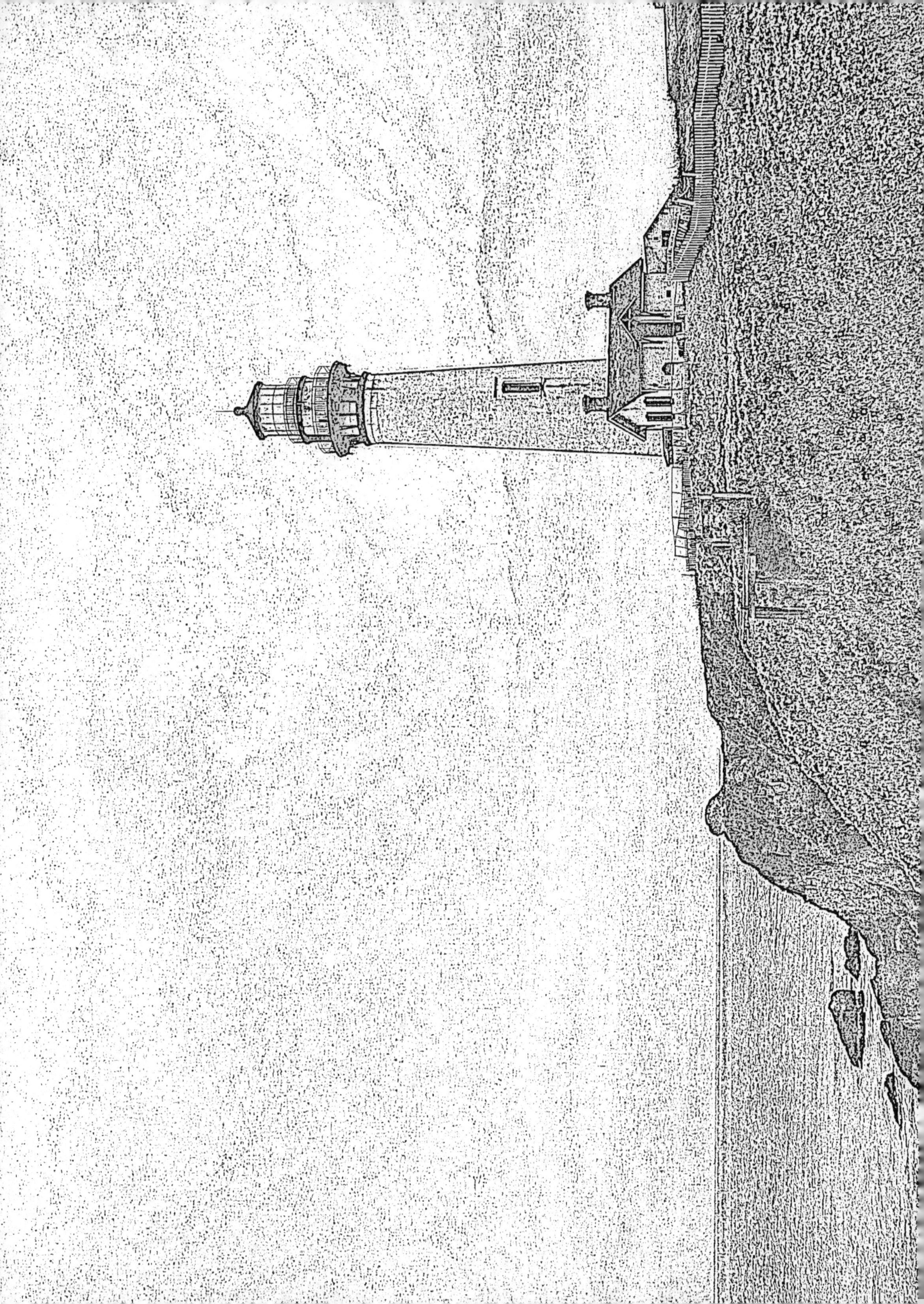

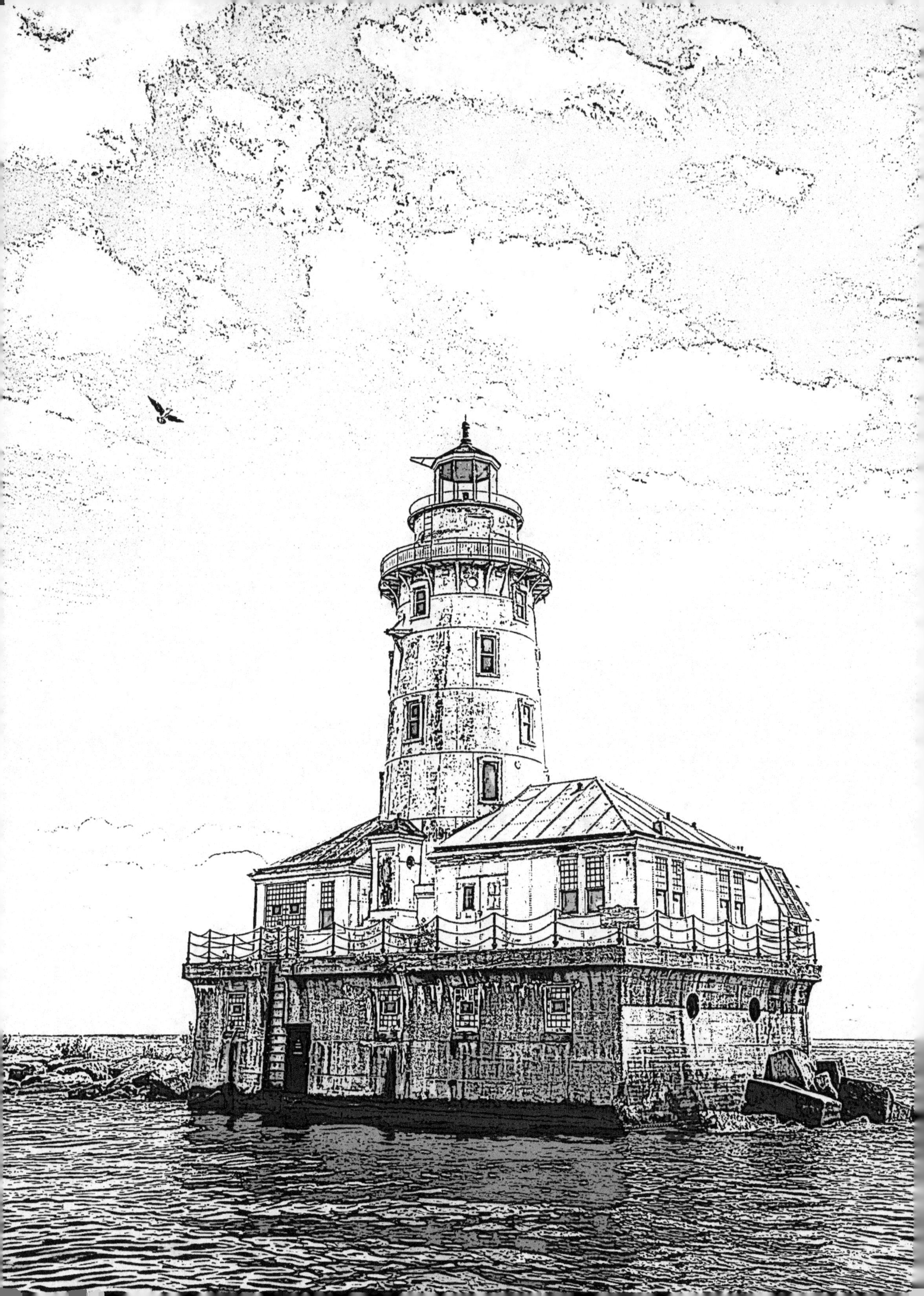

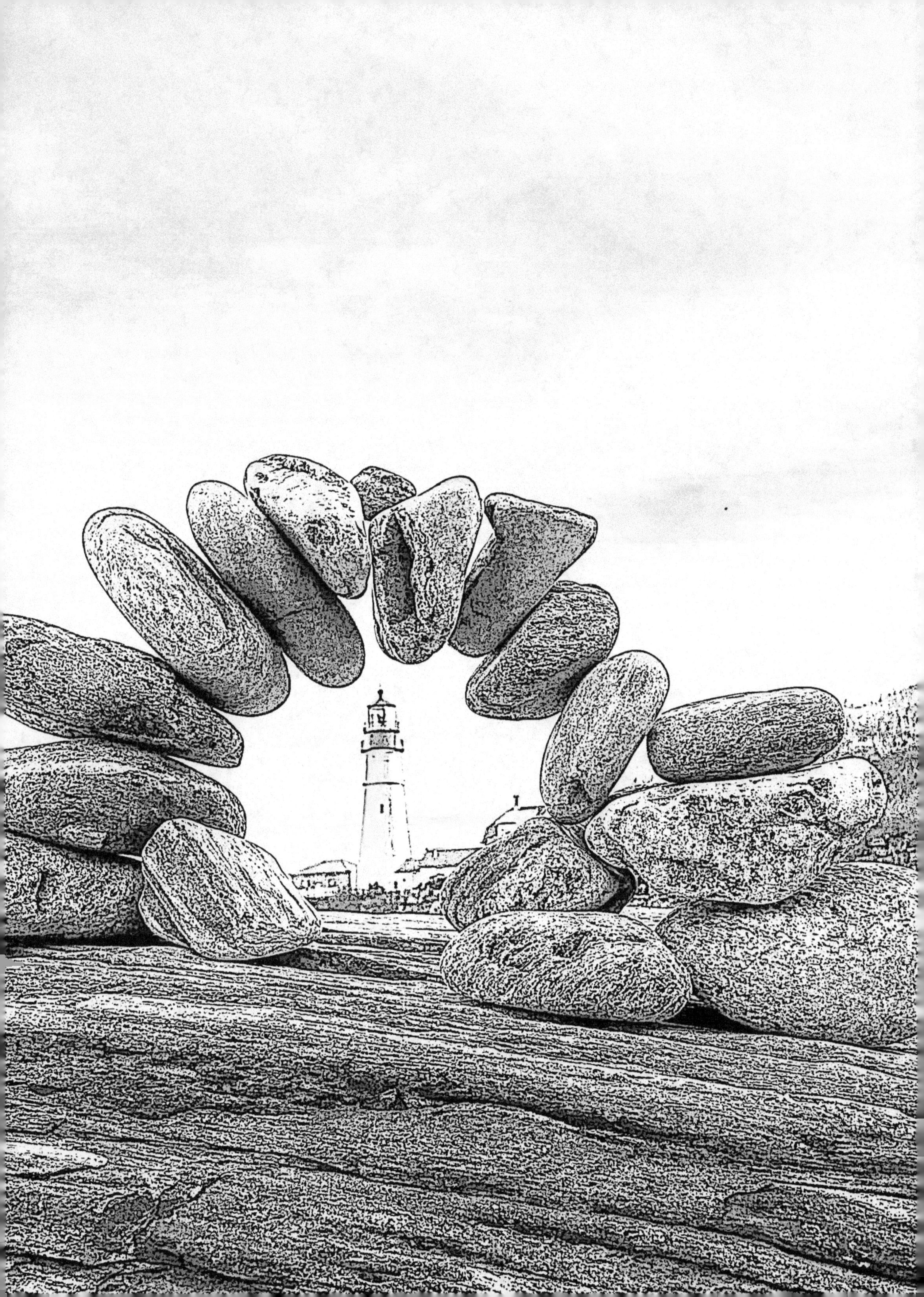

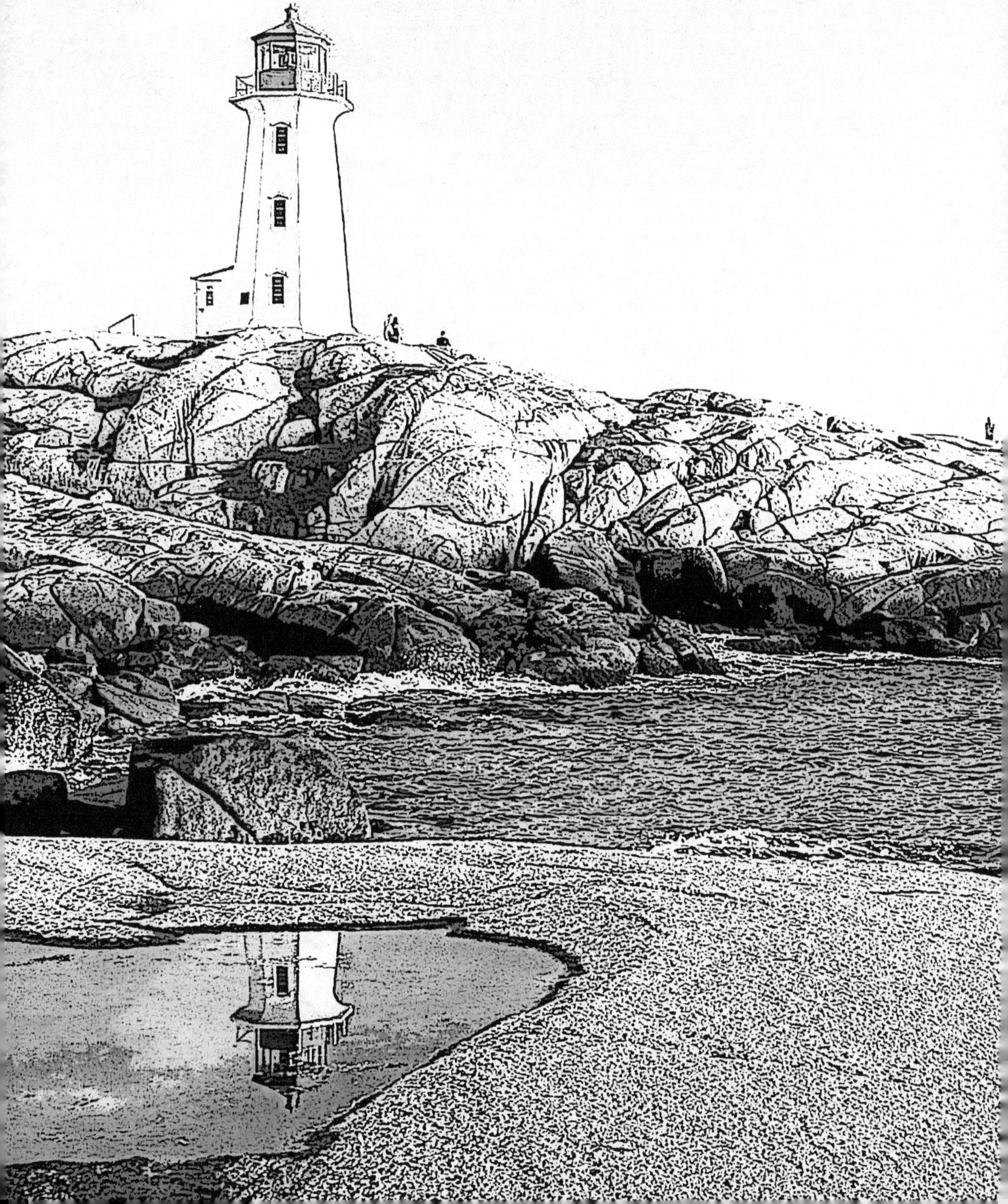

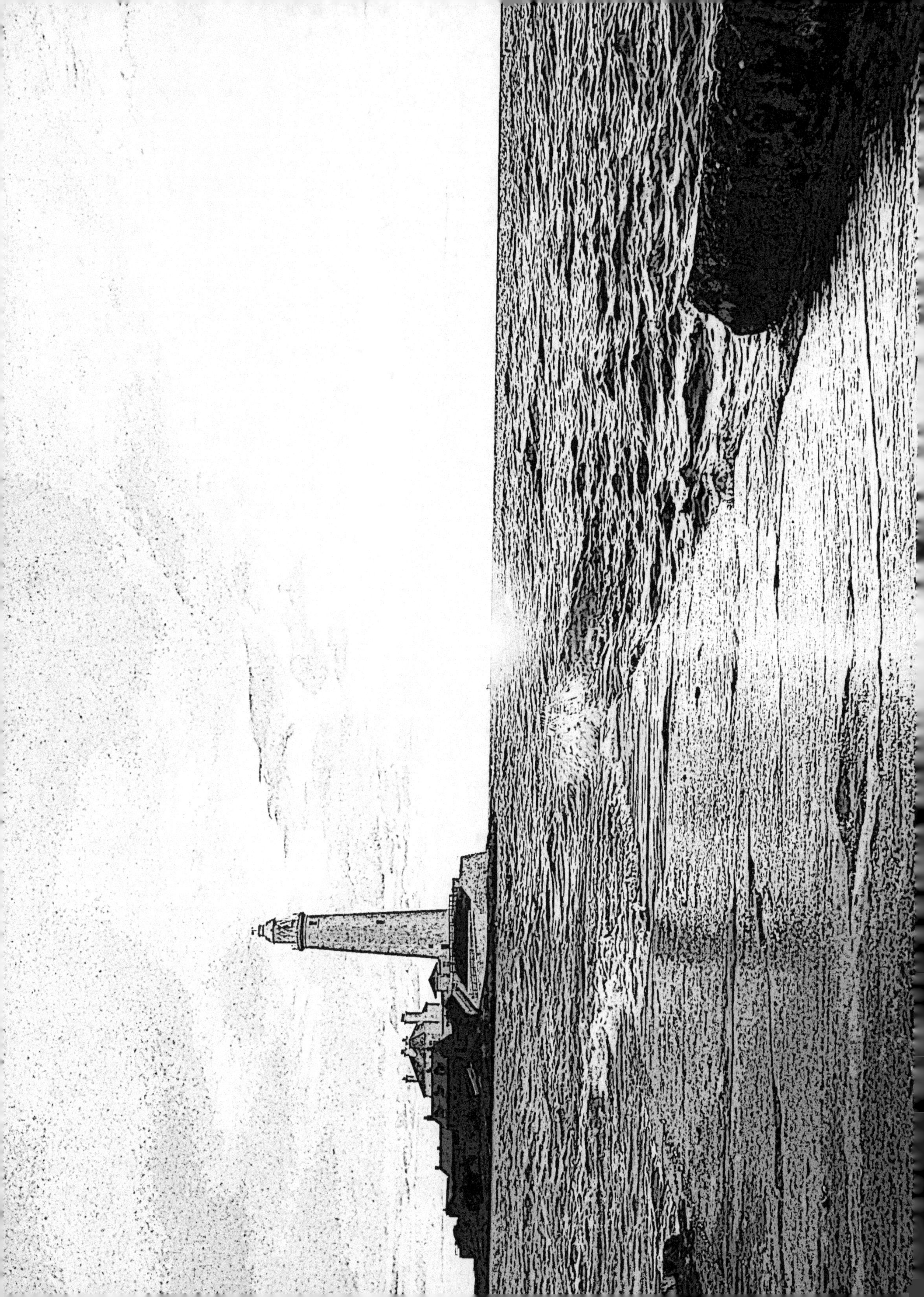

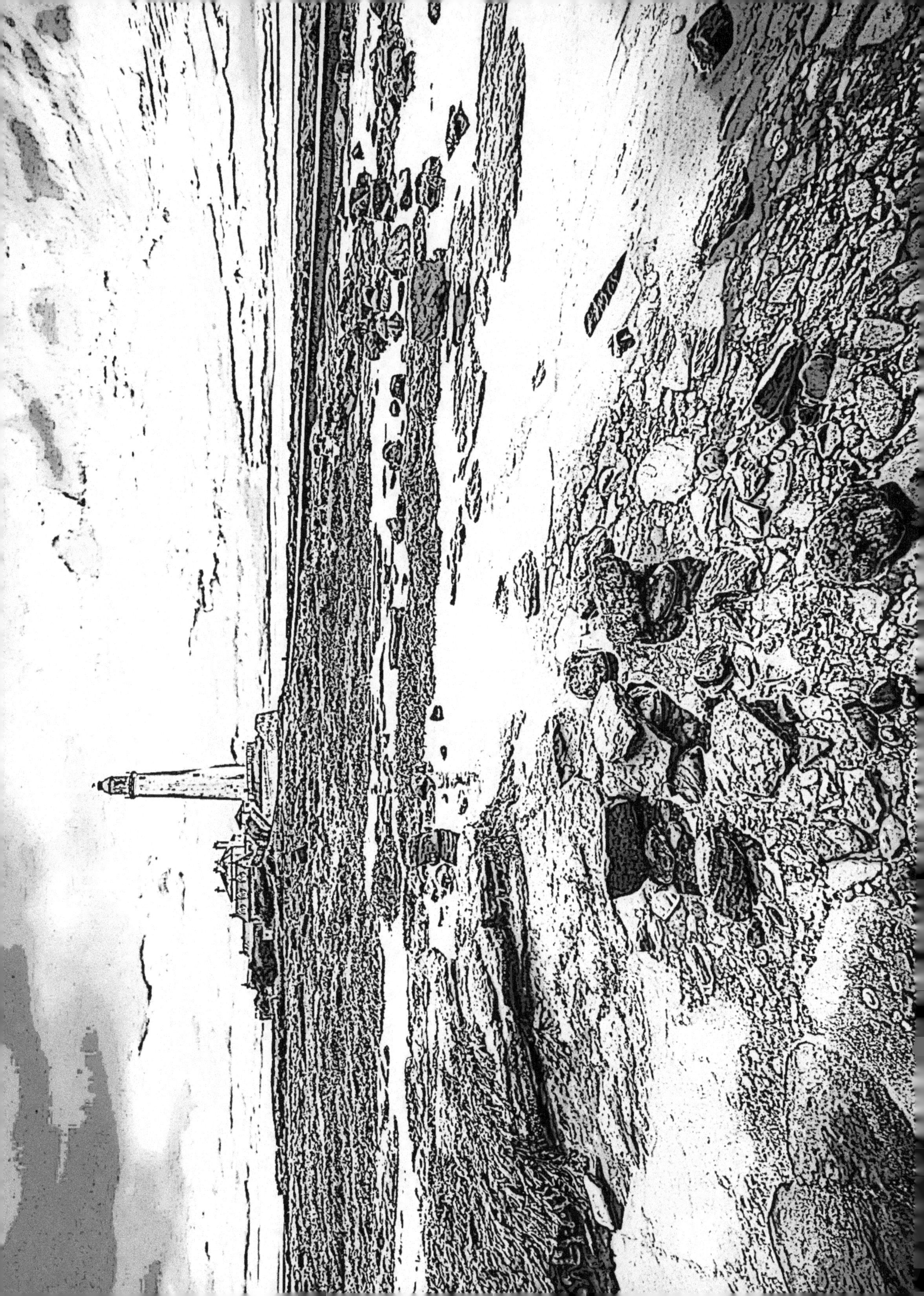

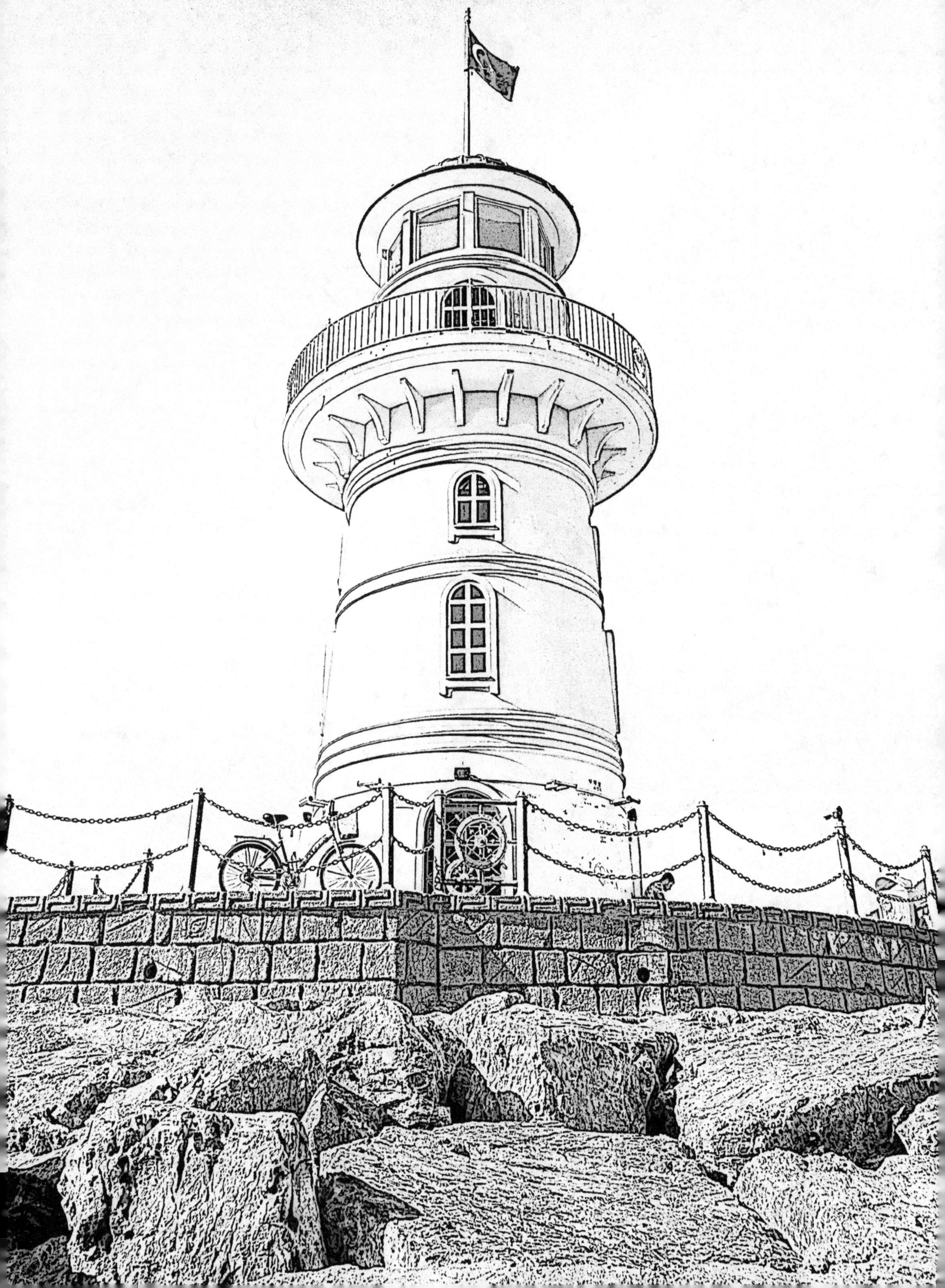

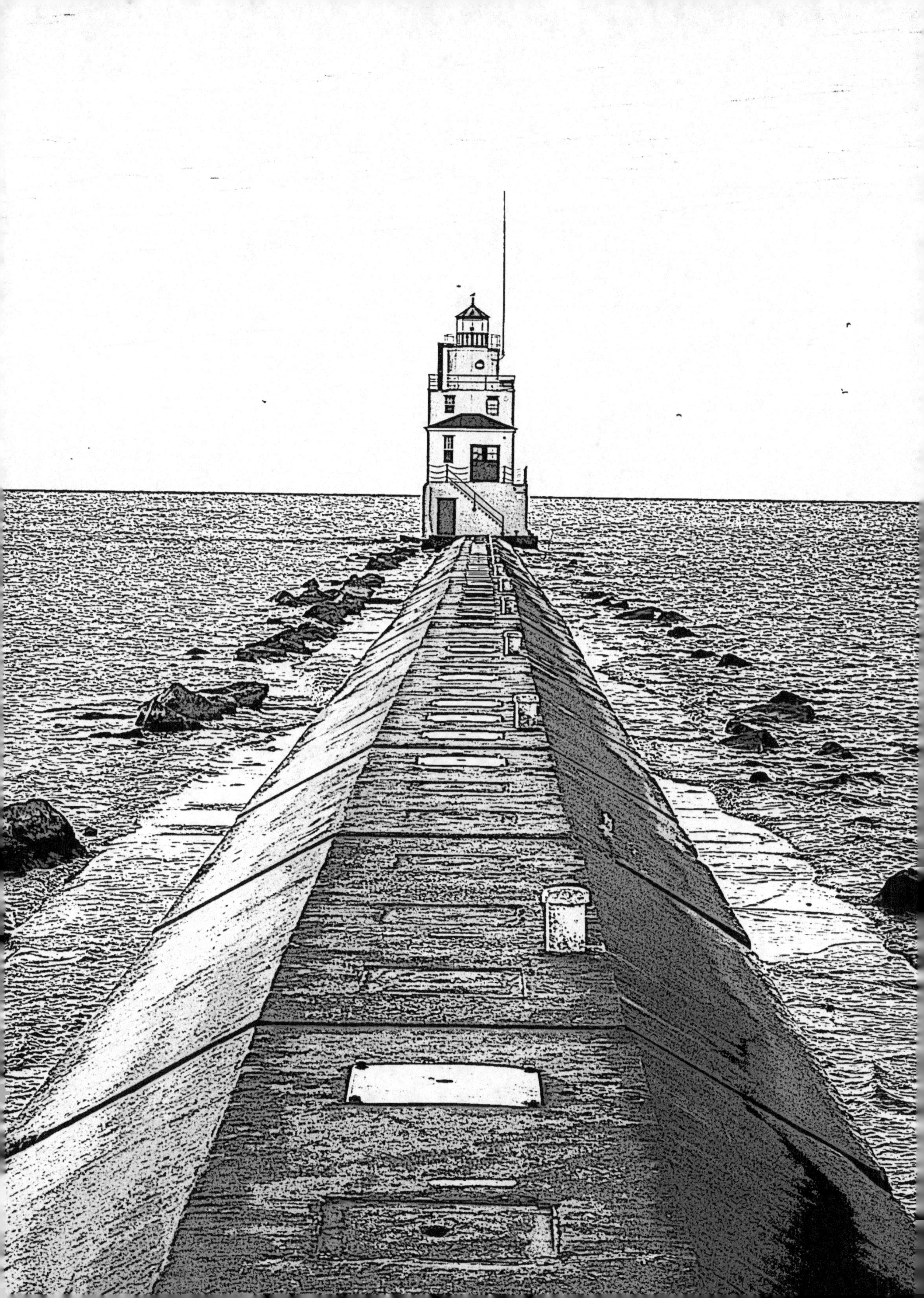

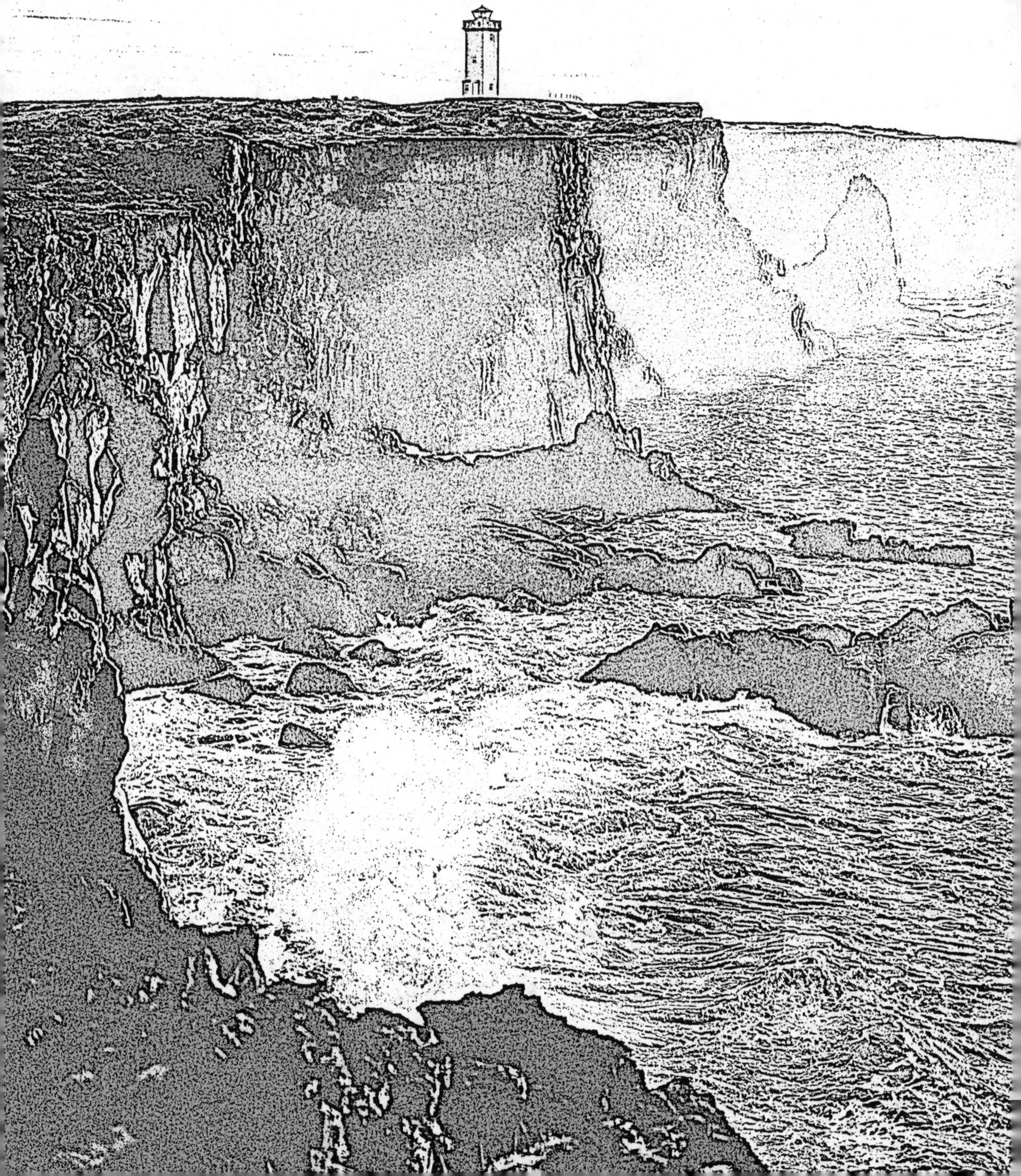

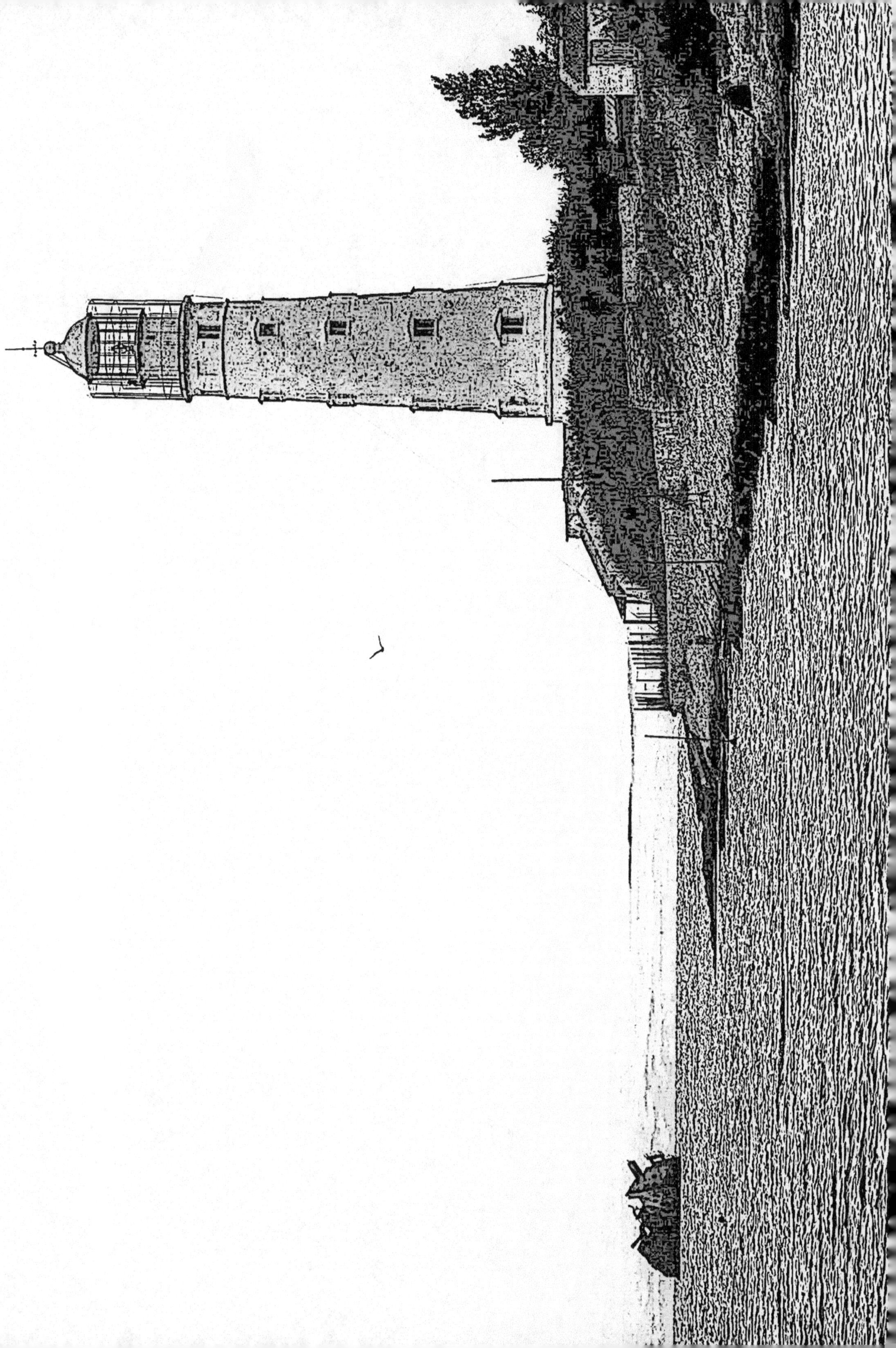

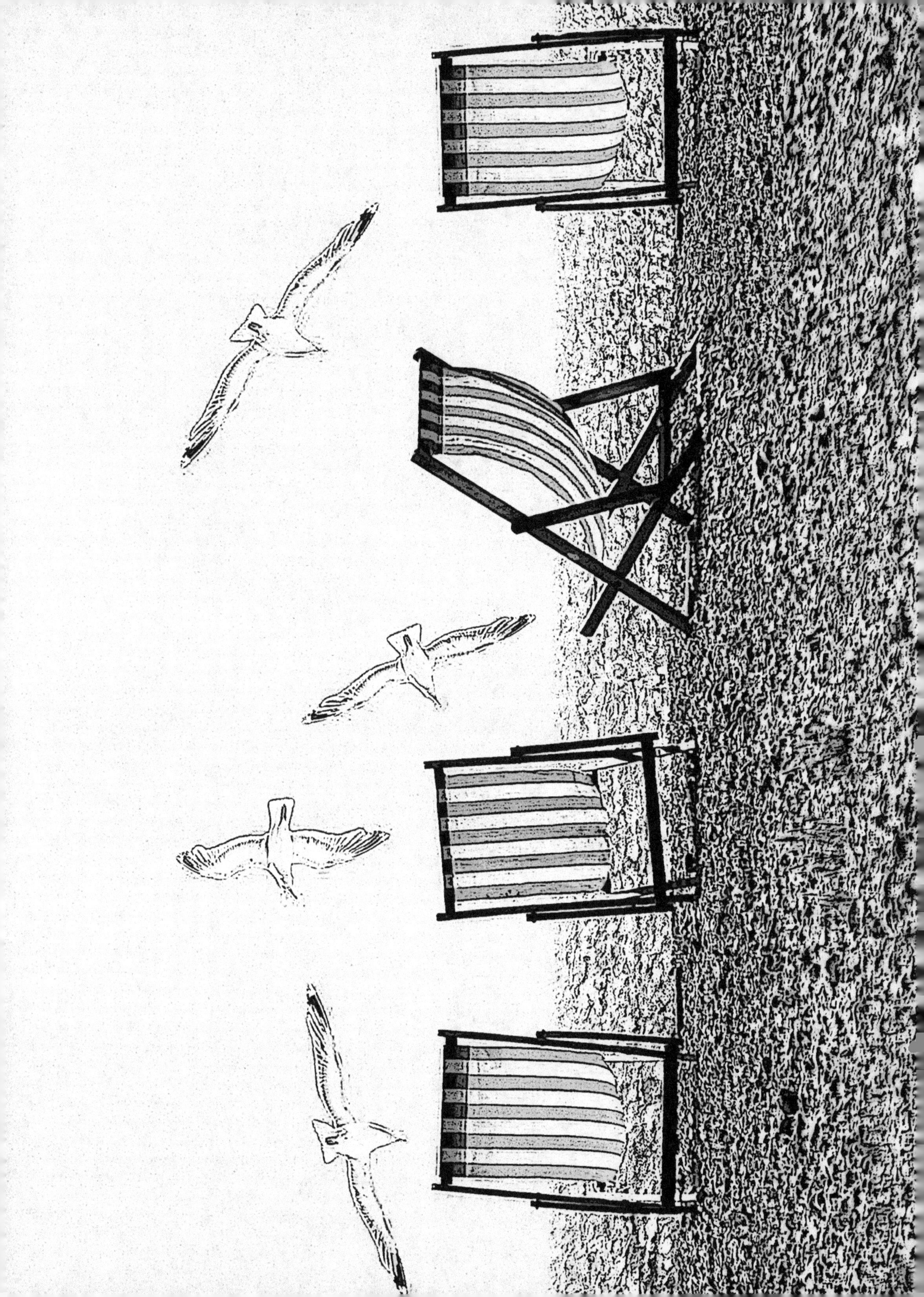

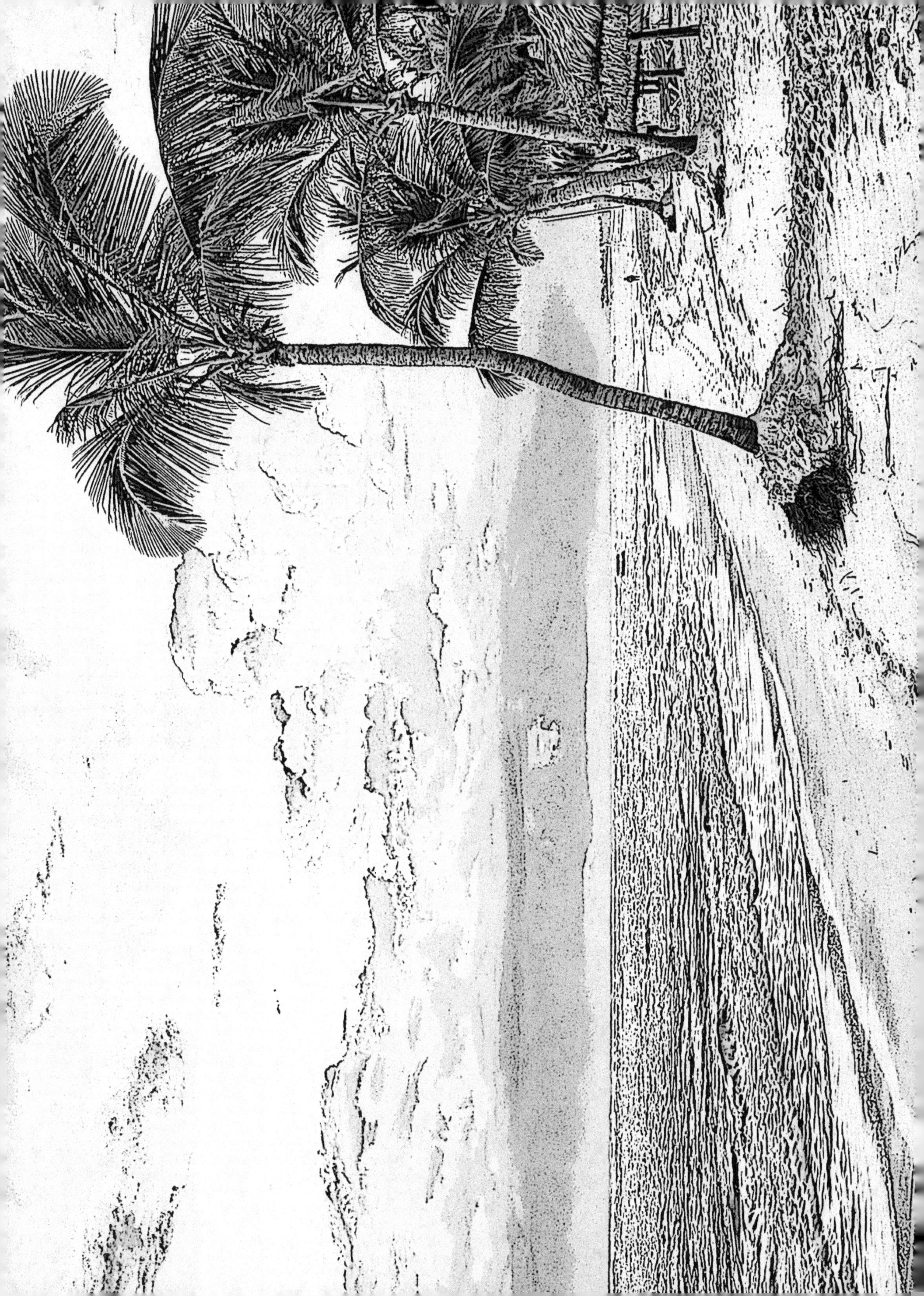

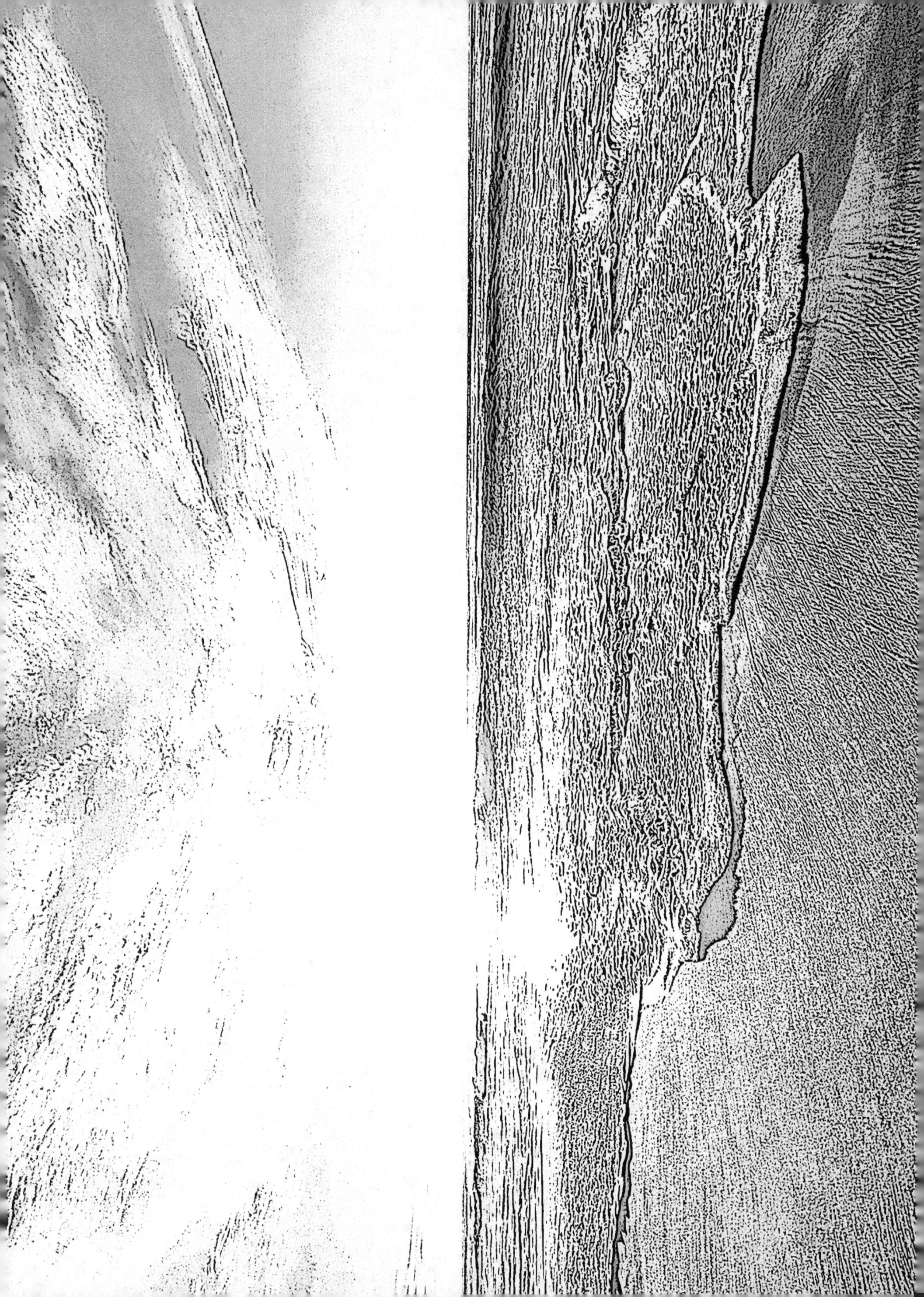

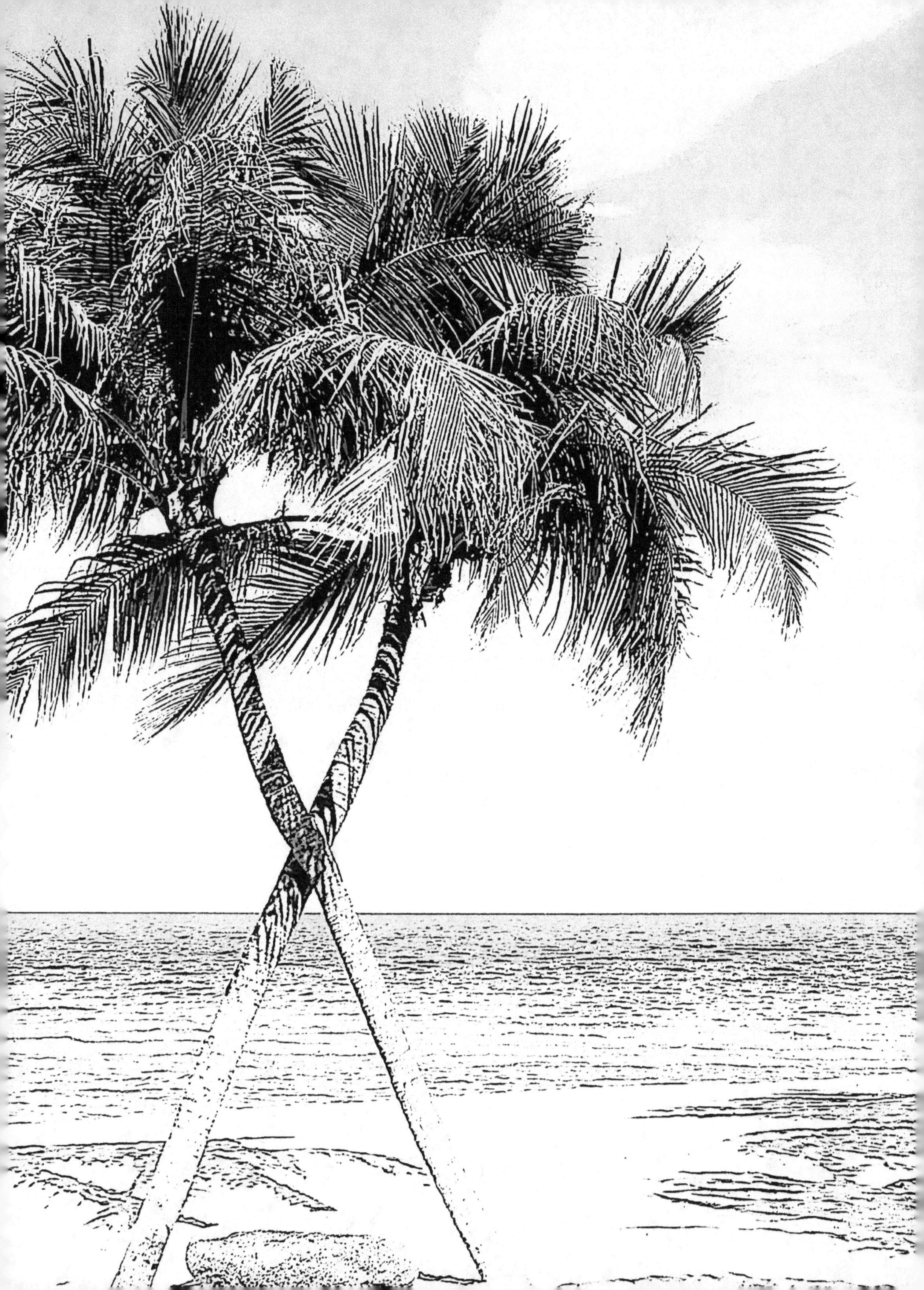

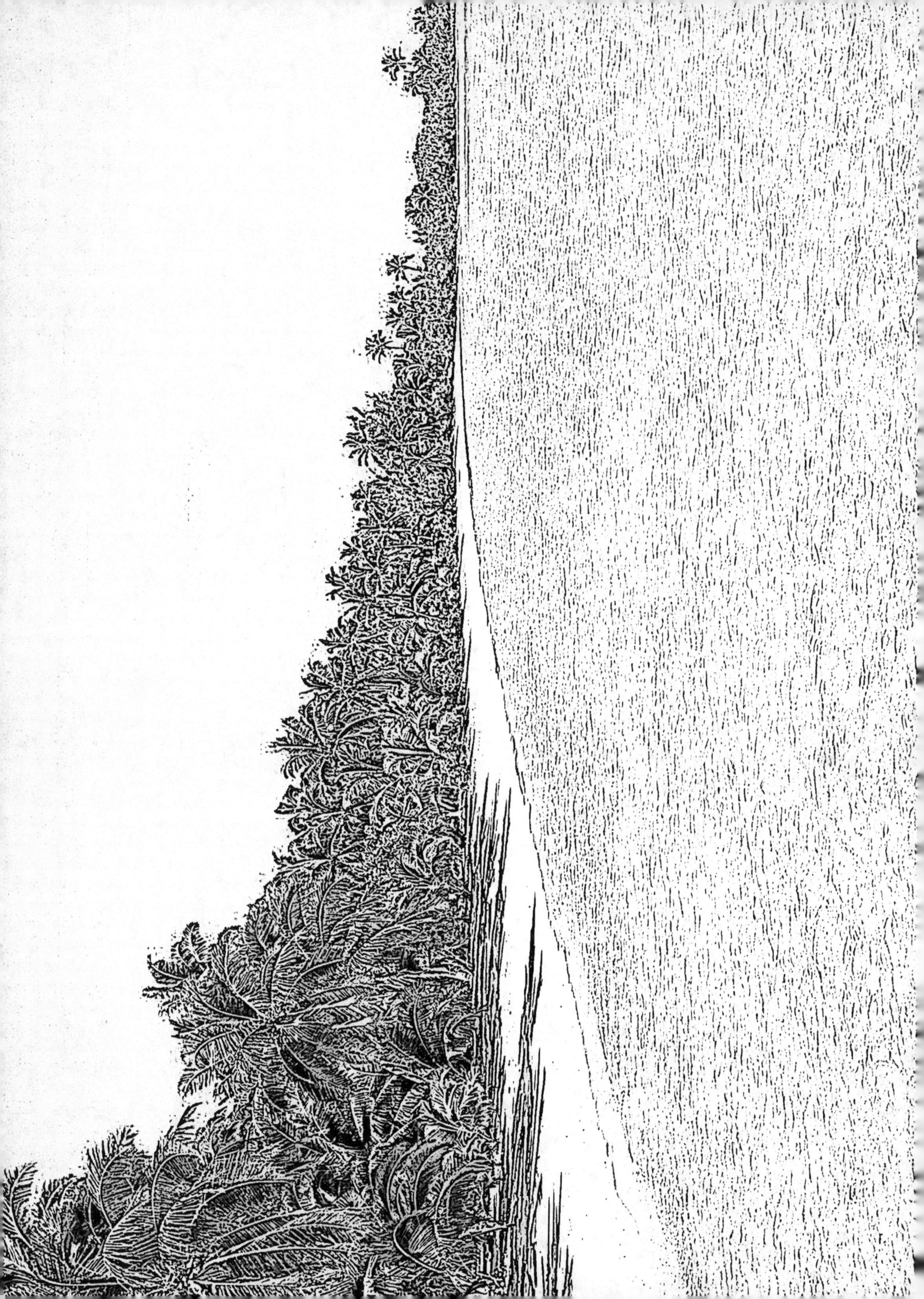

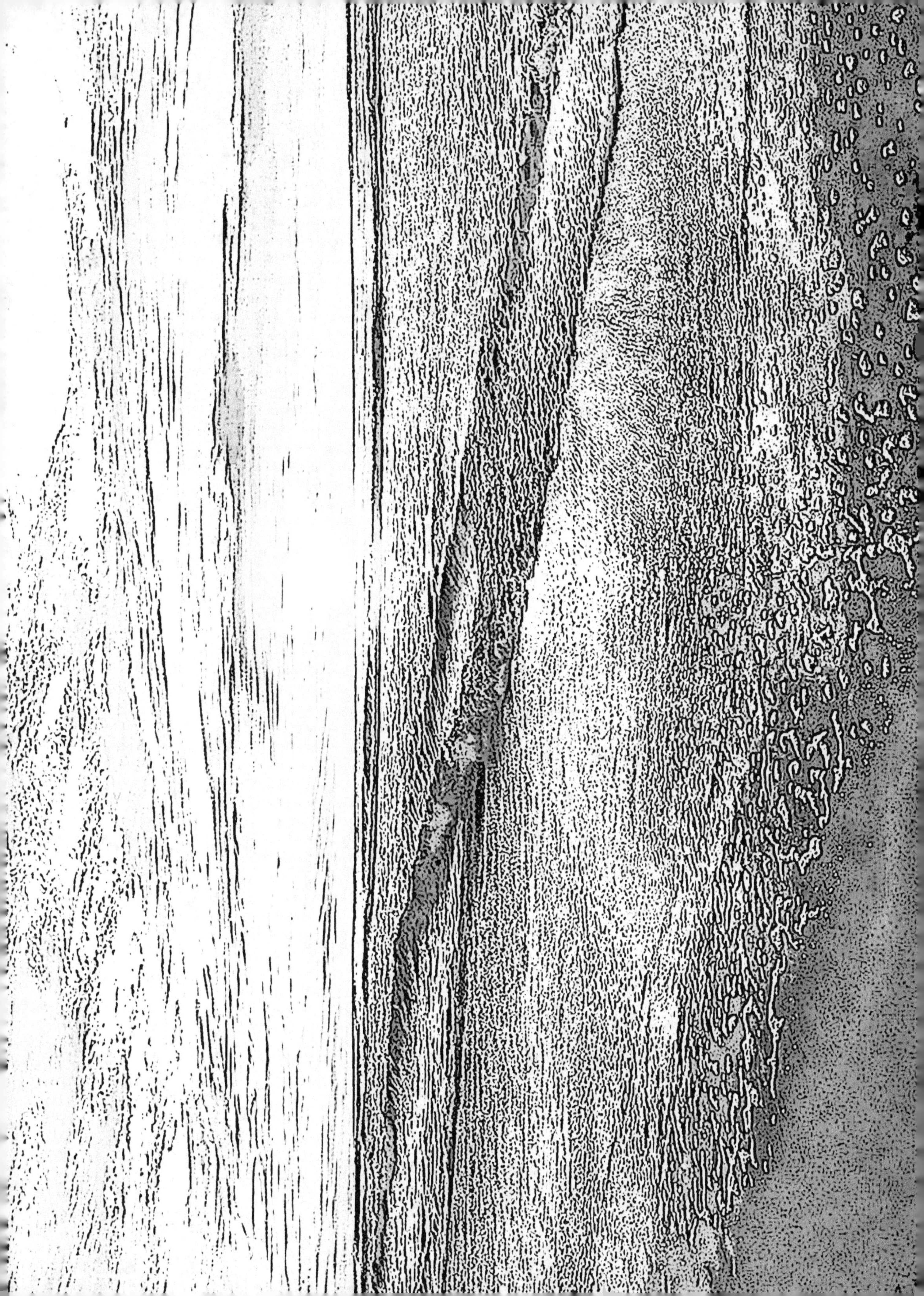

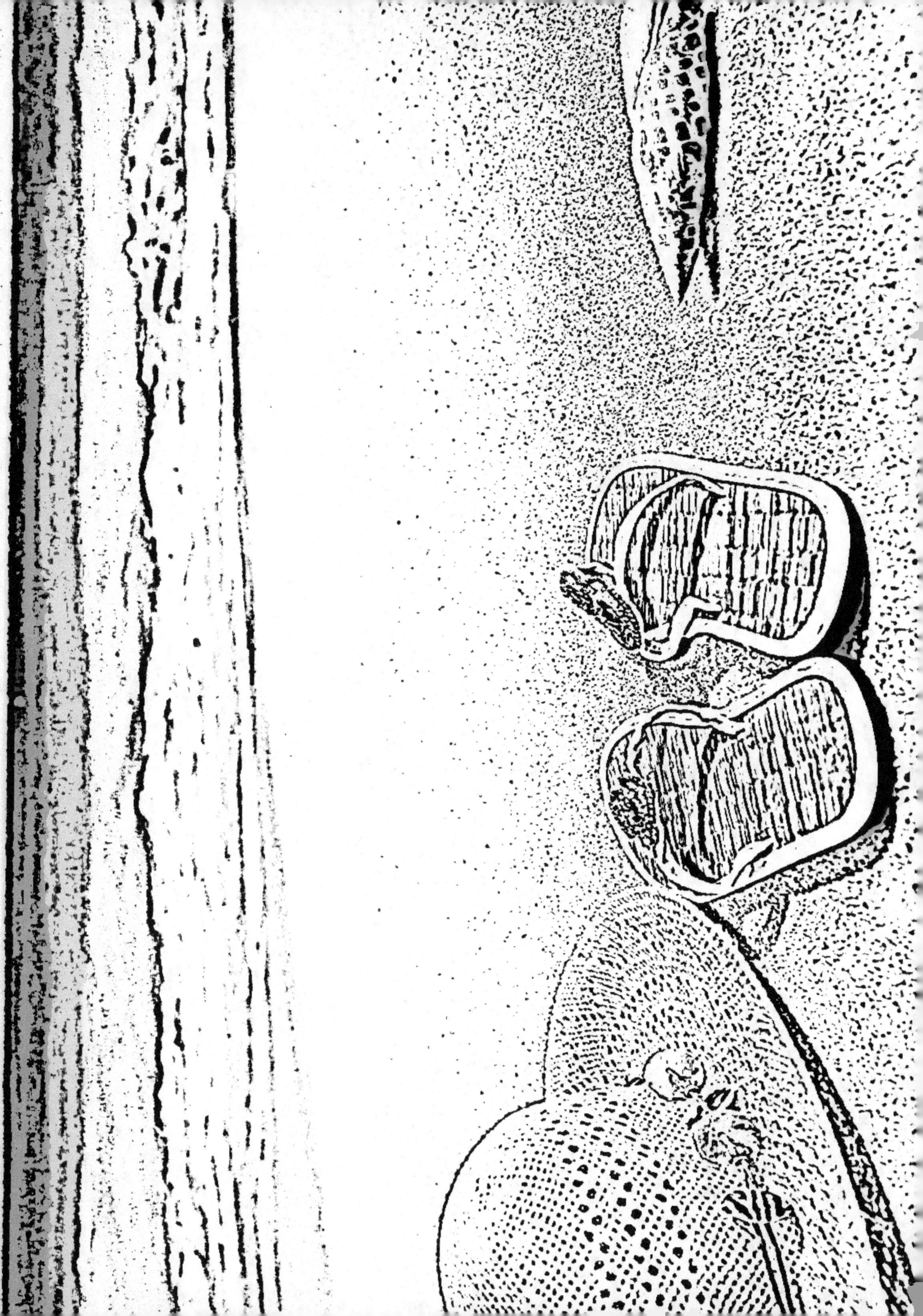

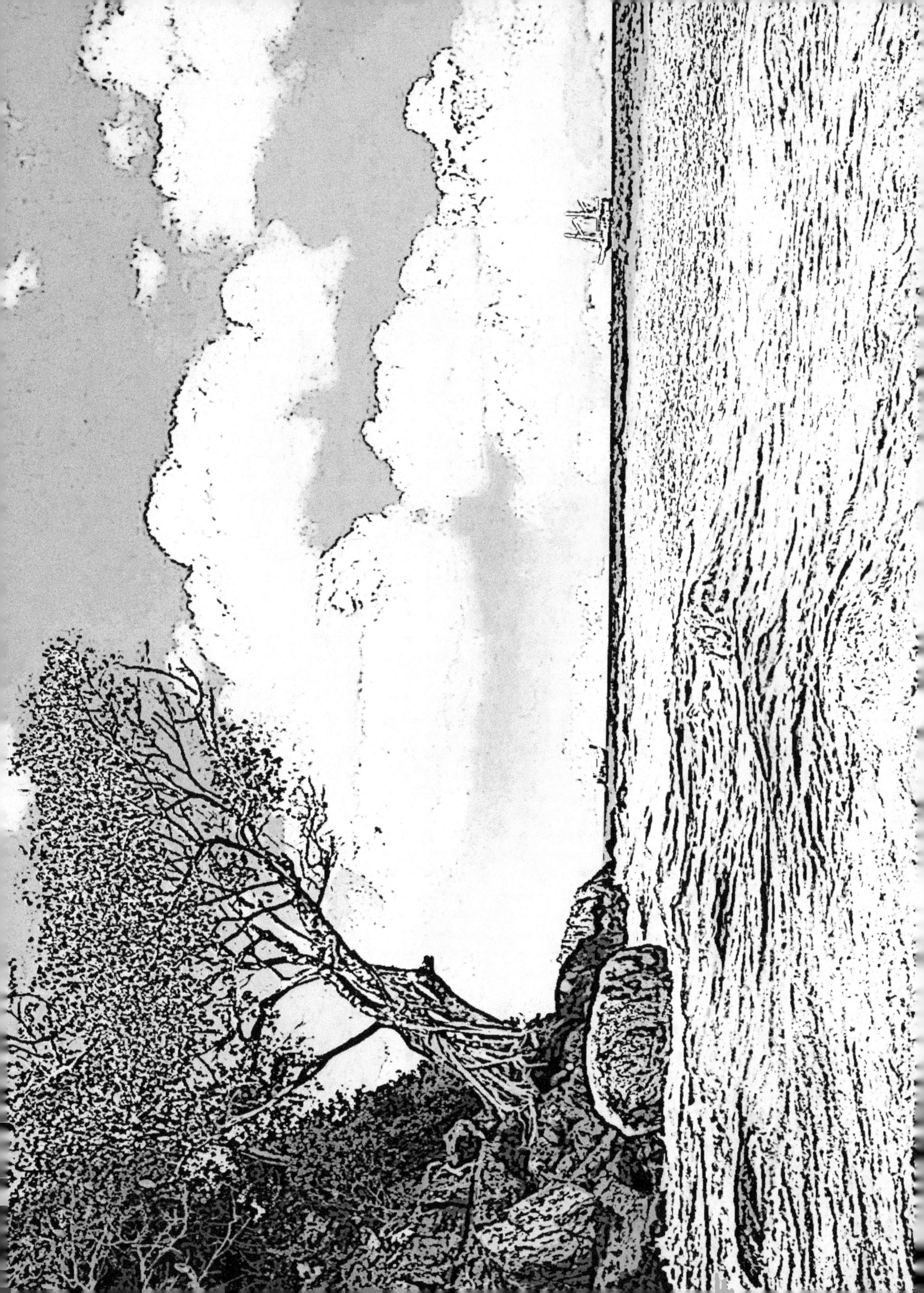

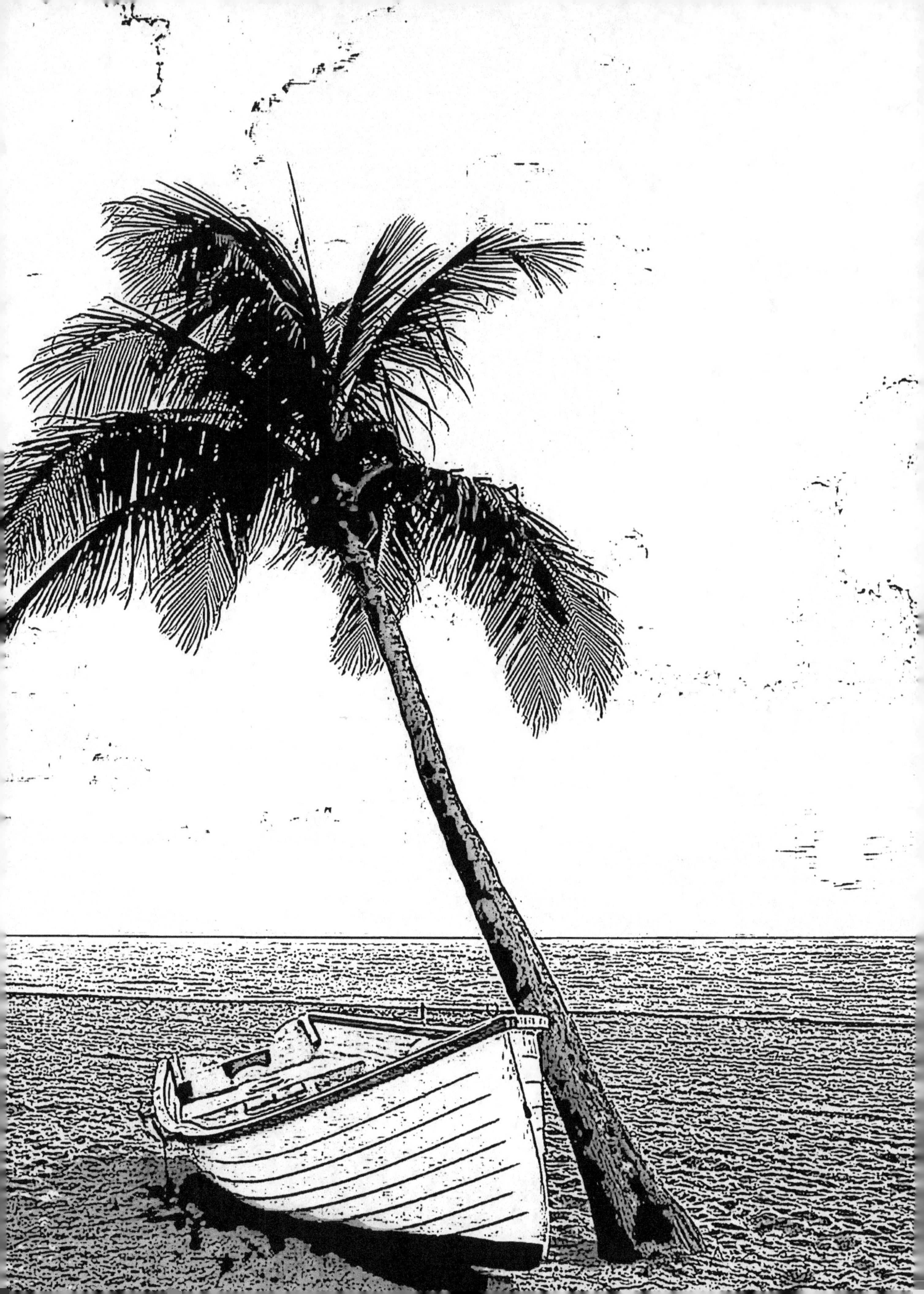

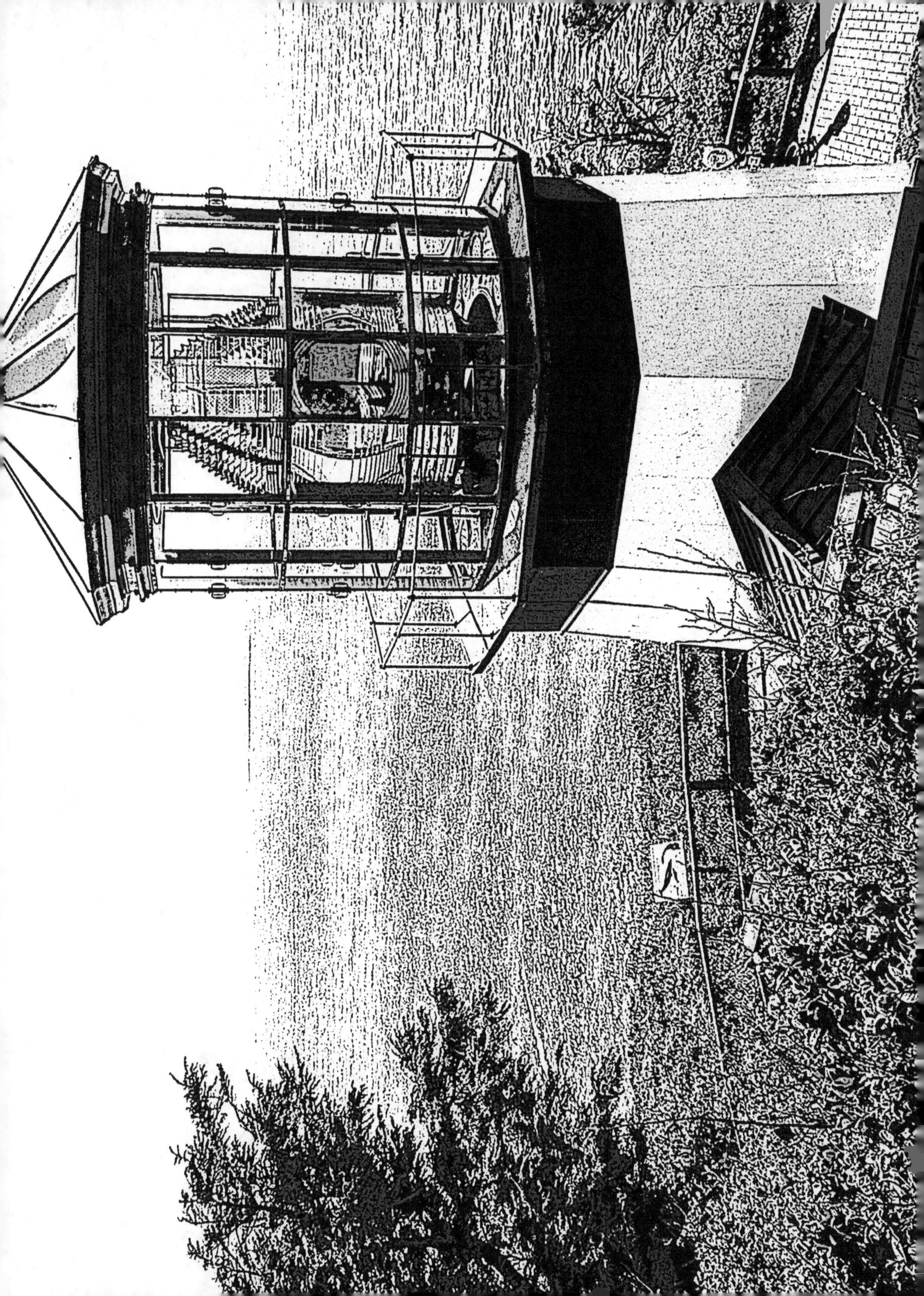

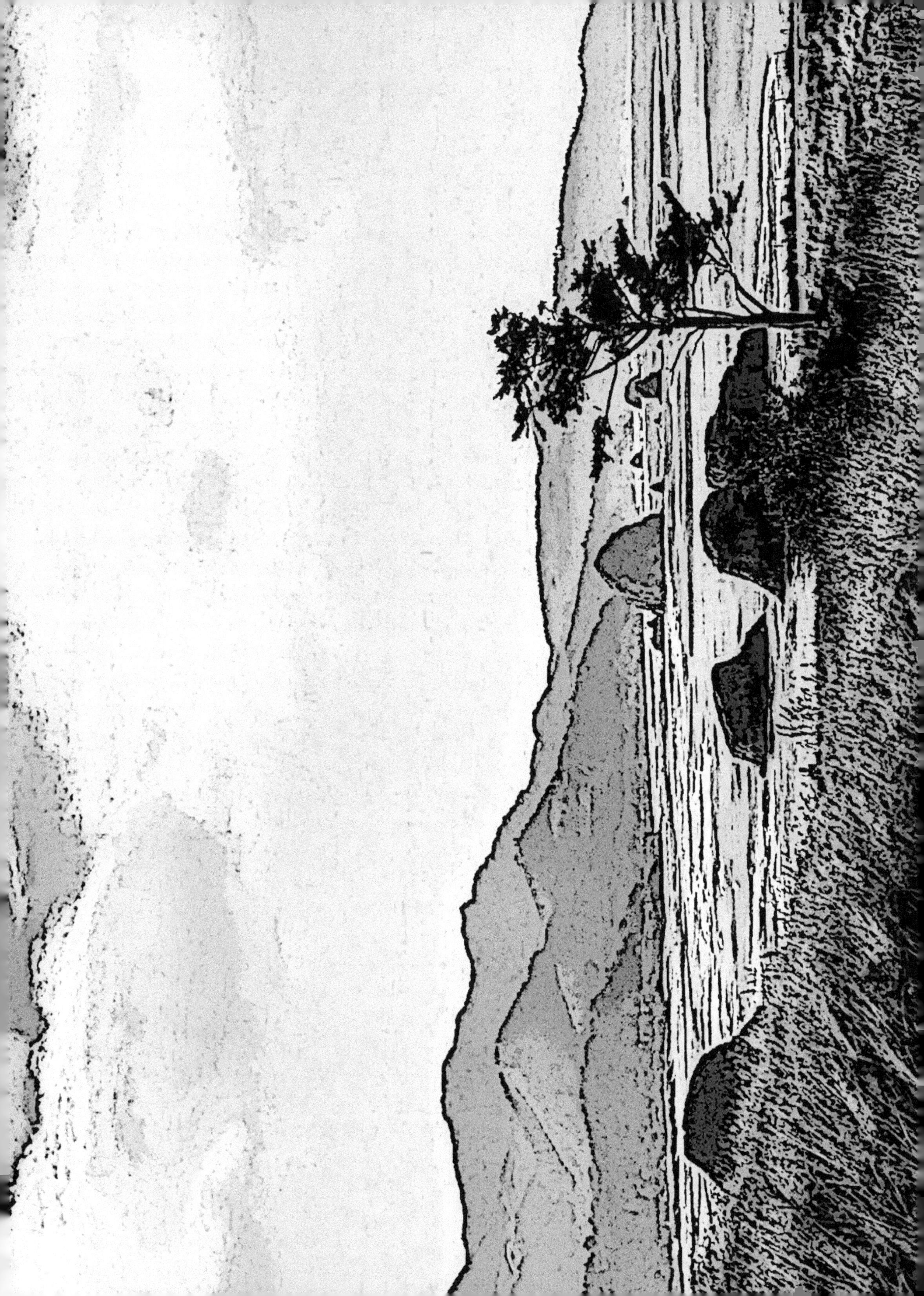

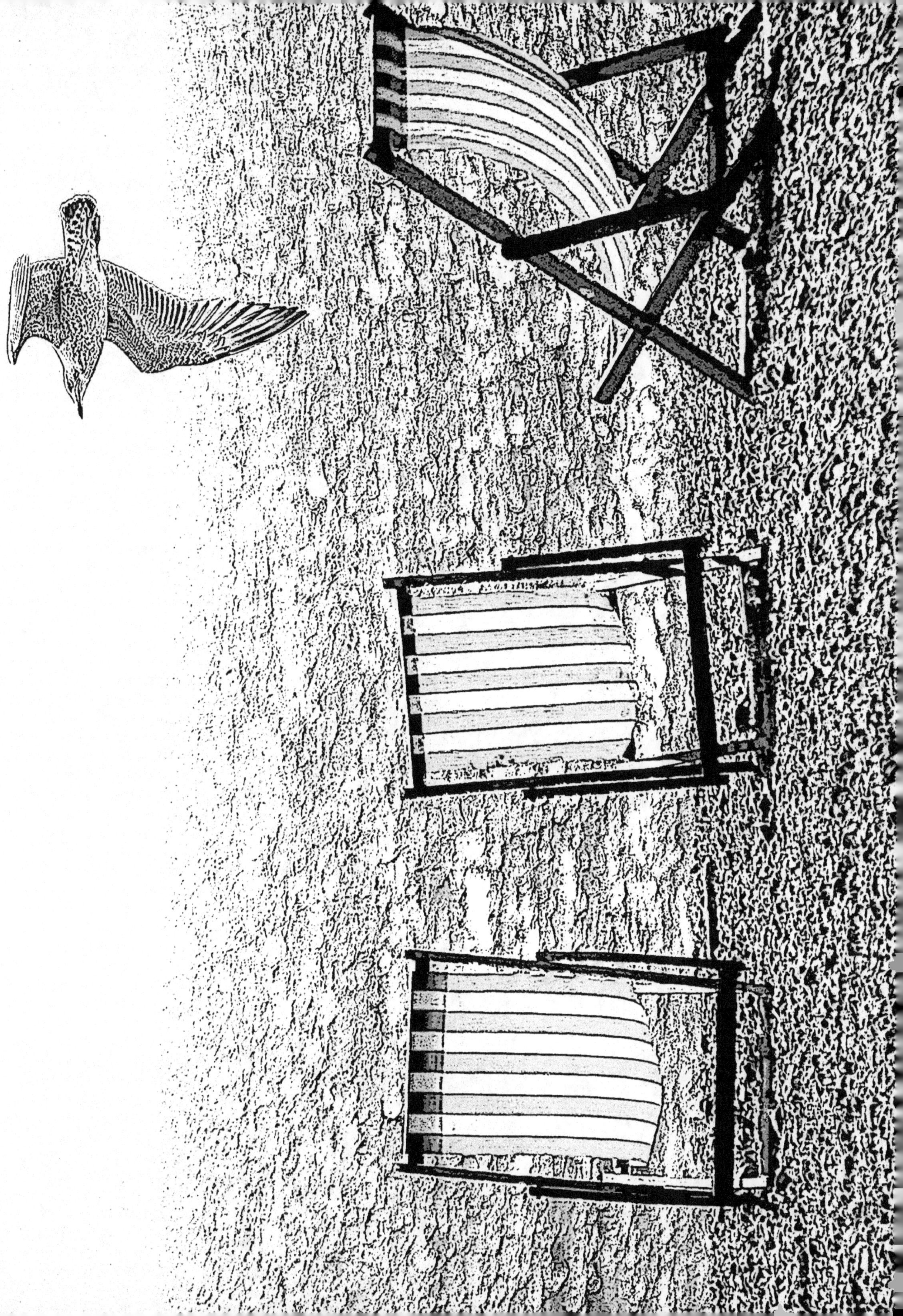

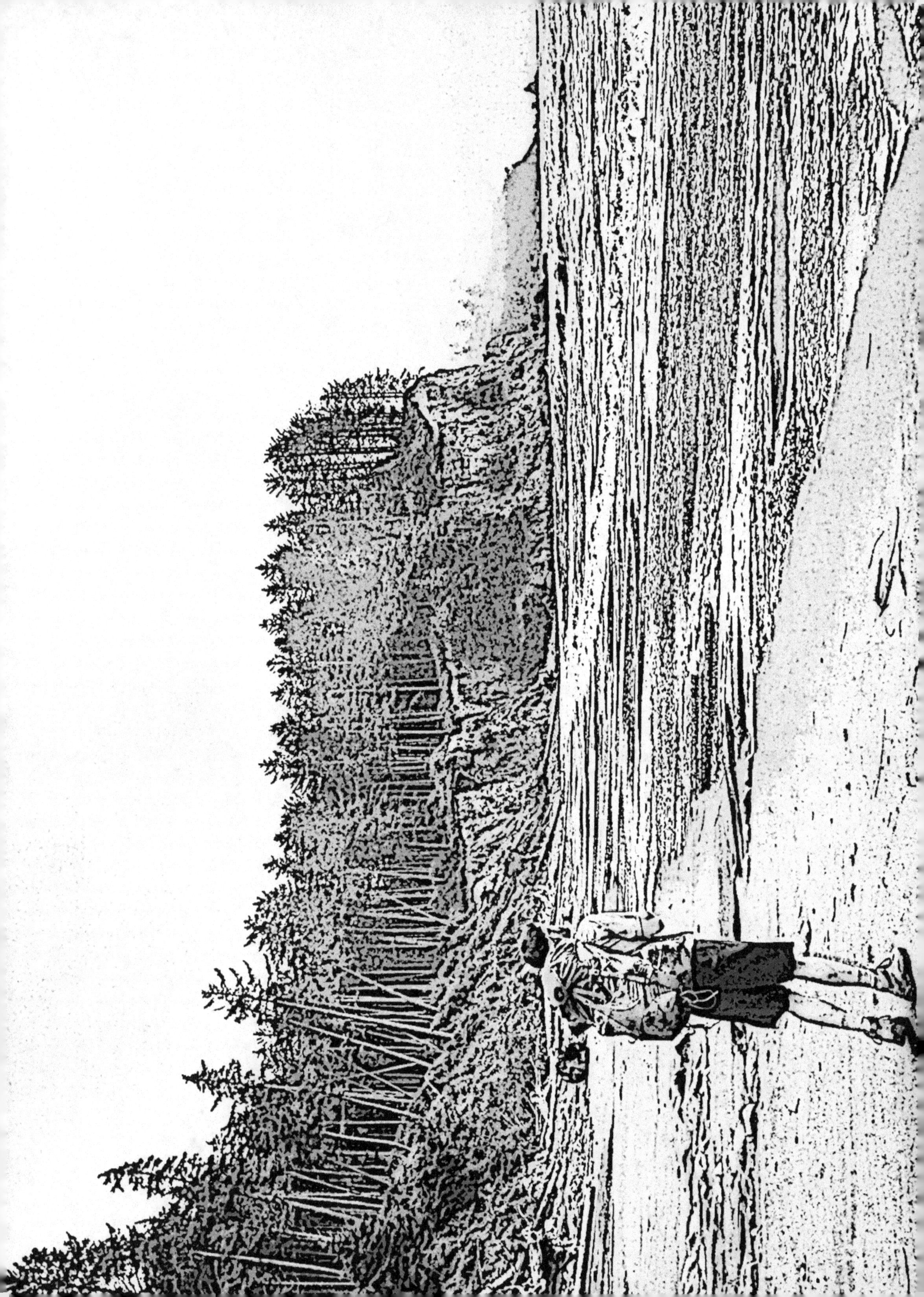

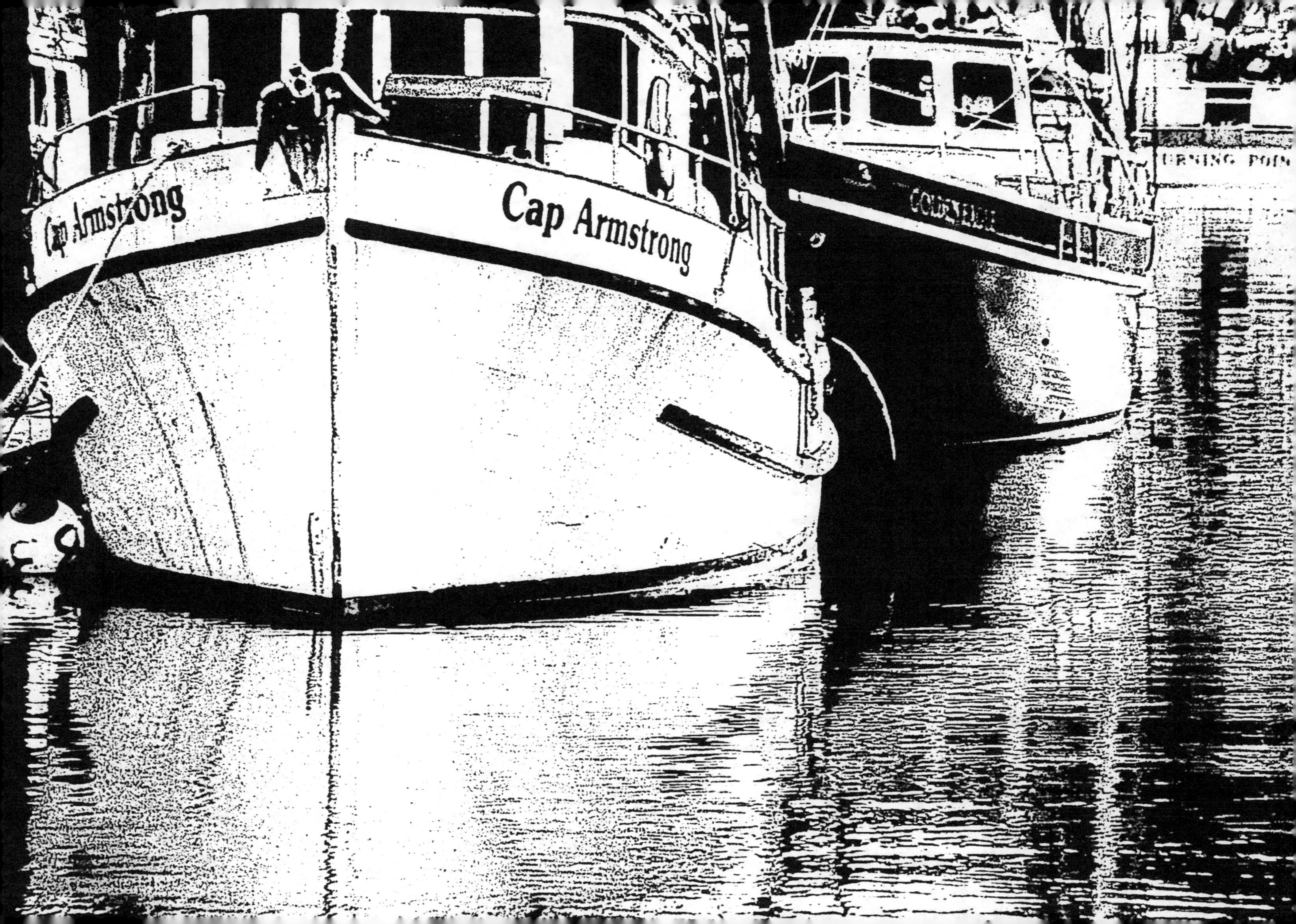
Cap Armstrong
Cap Armstrong

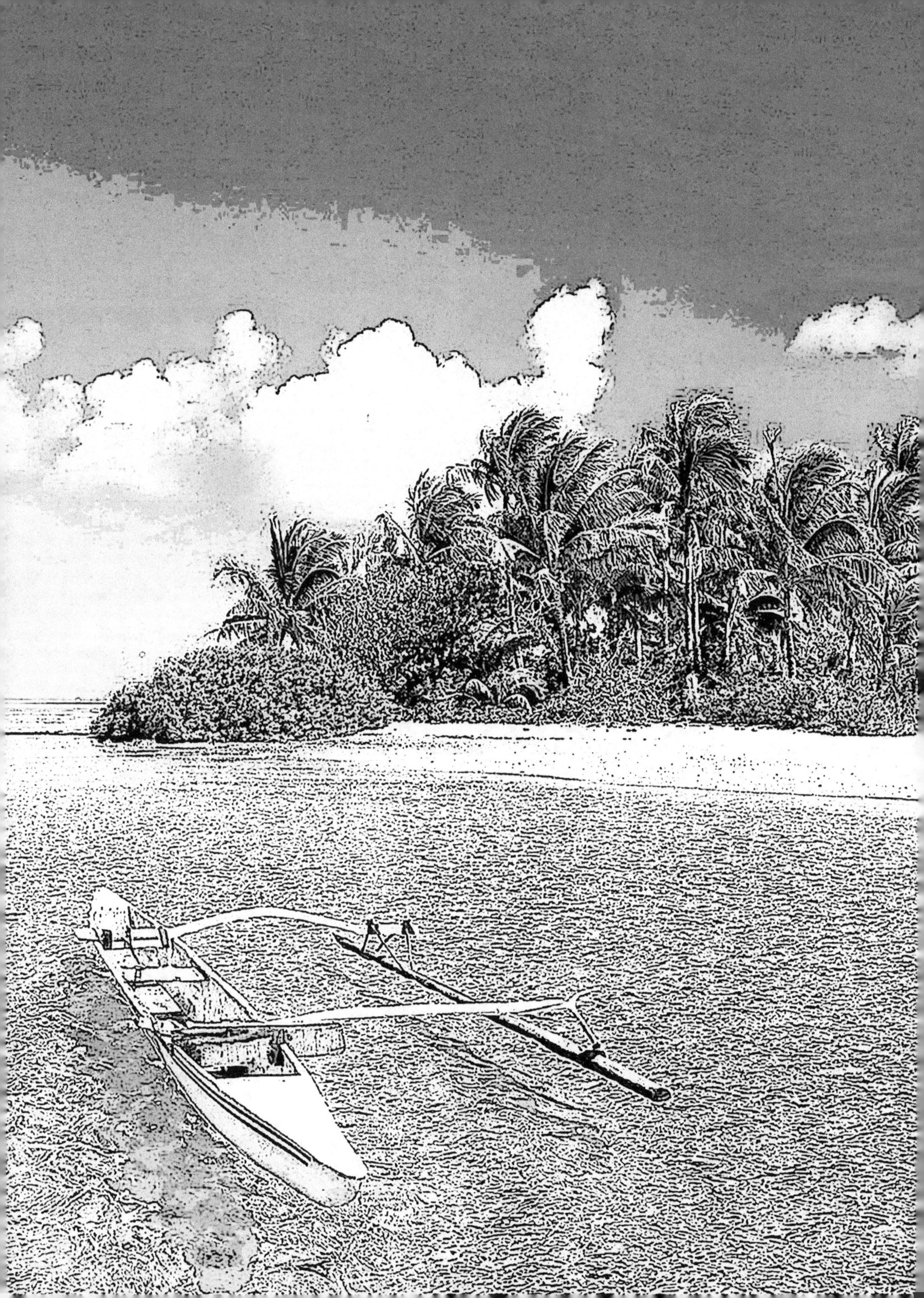

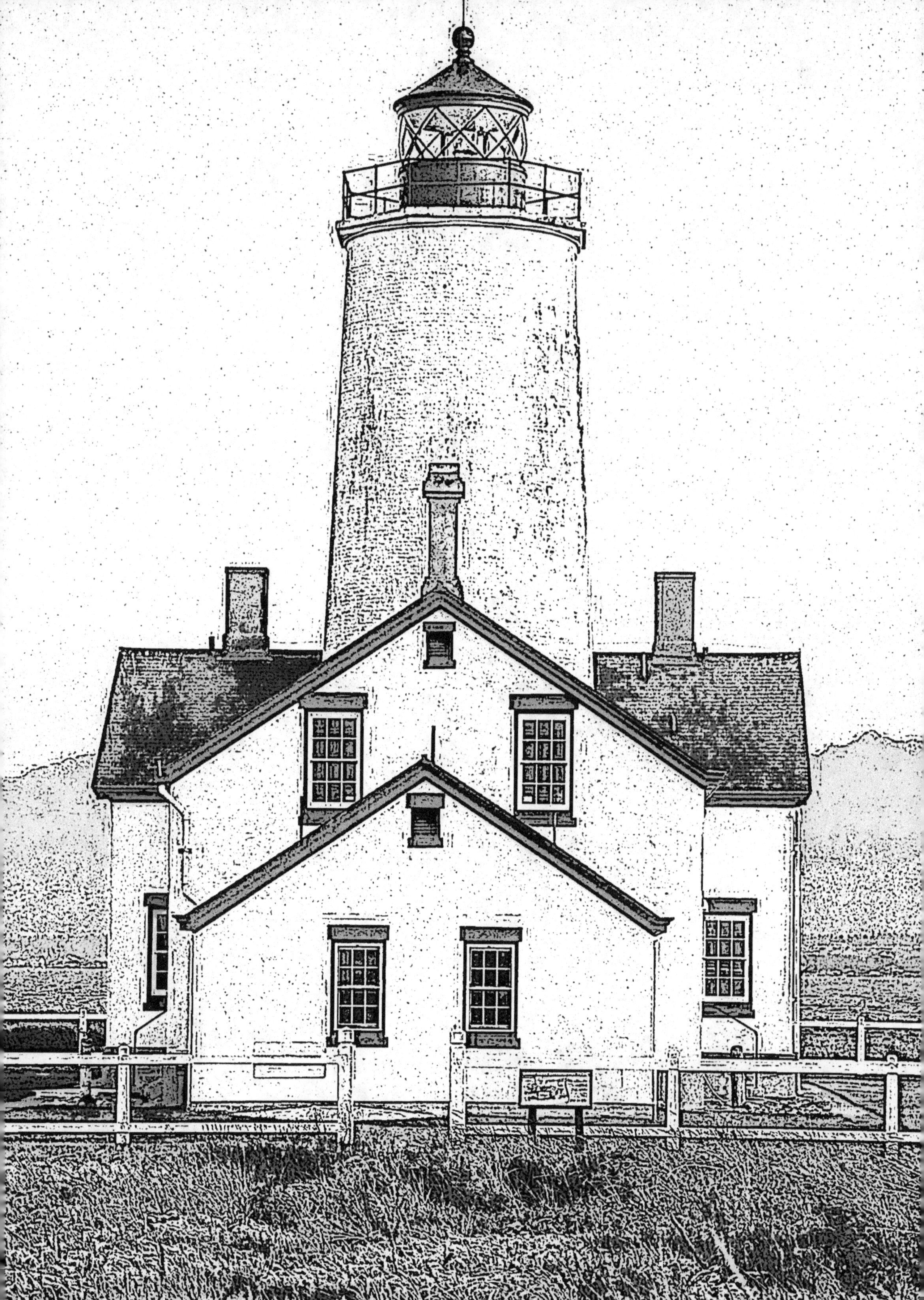

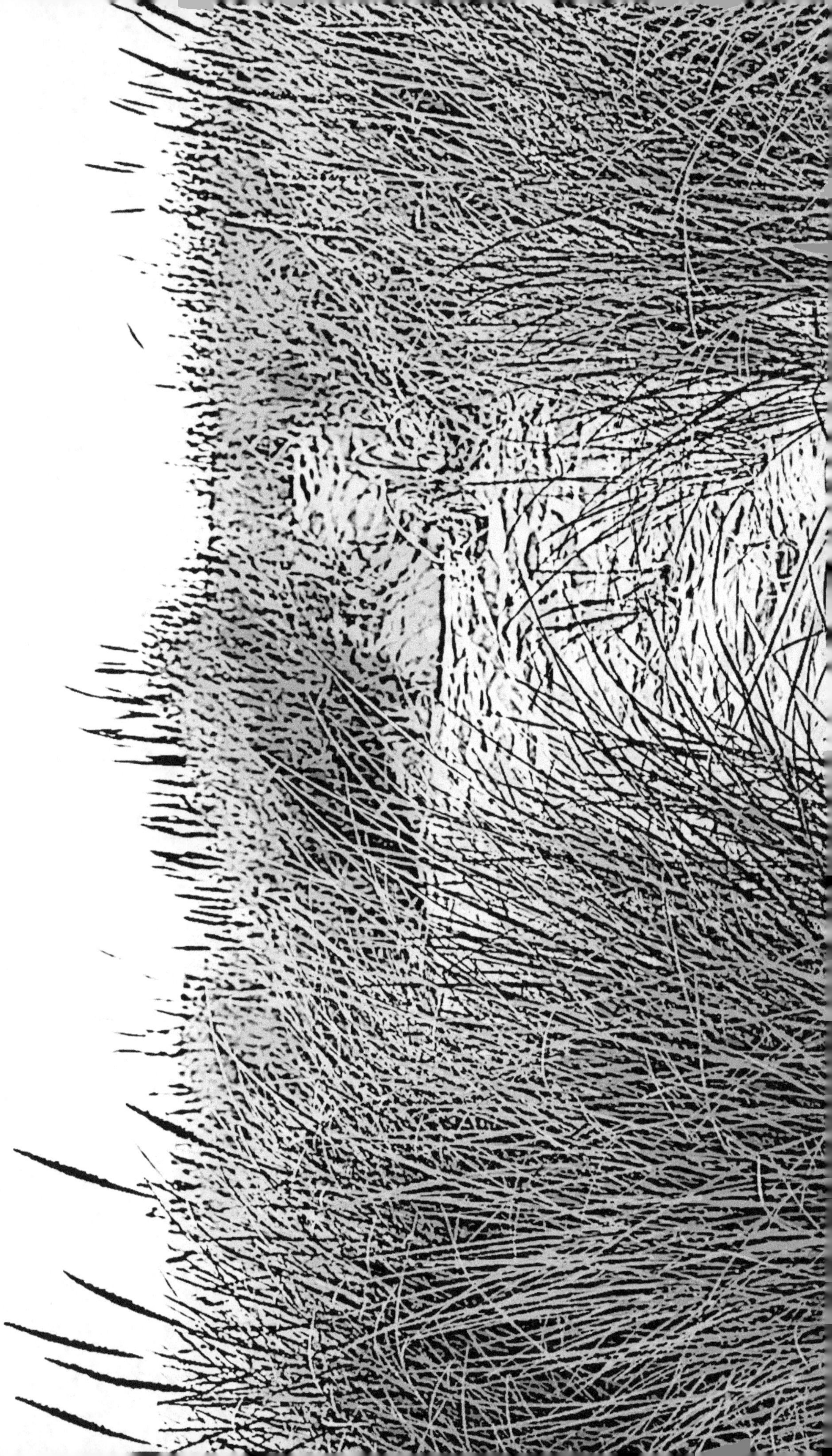

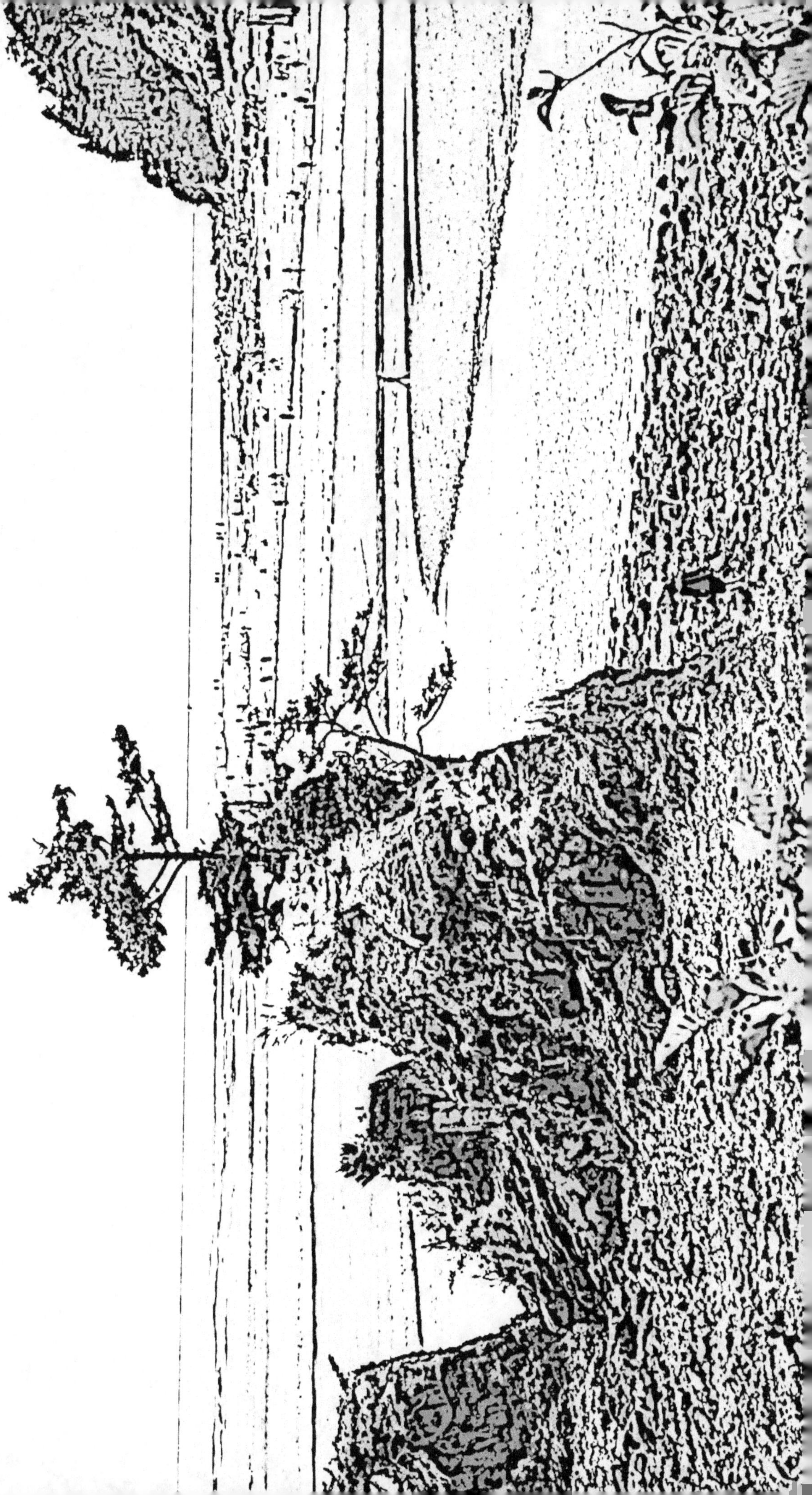

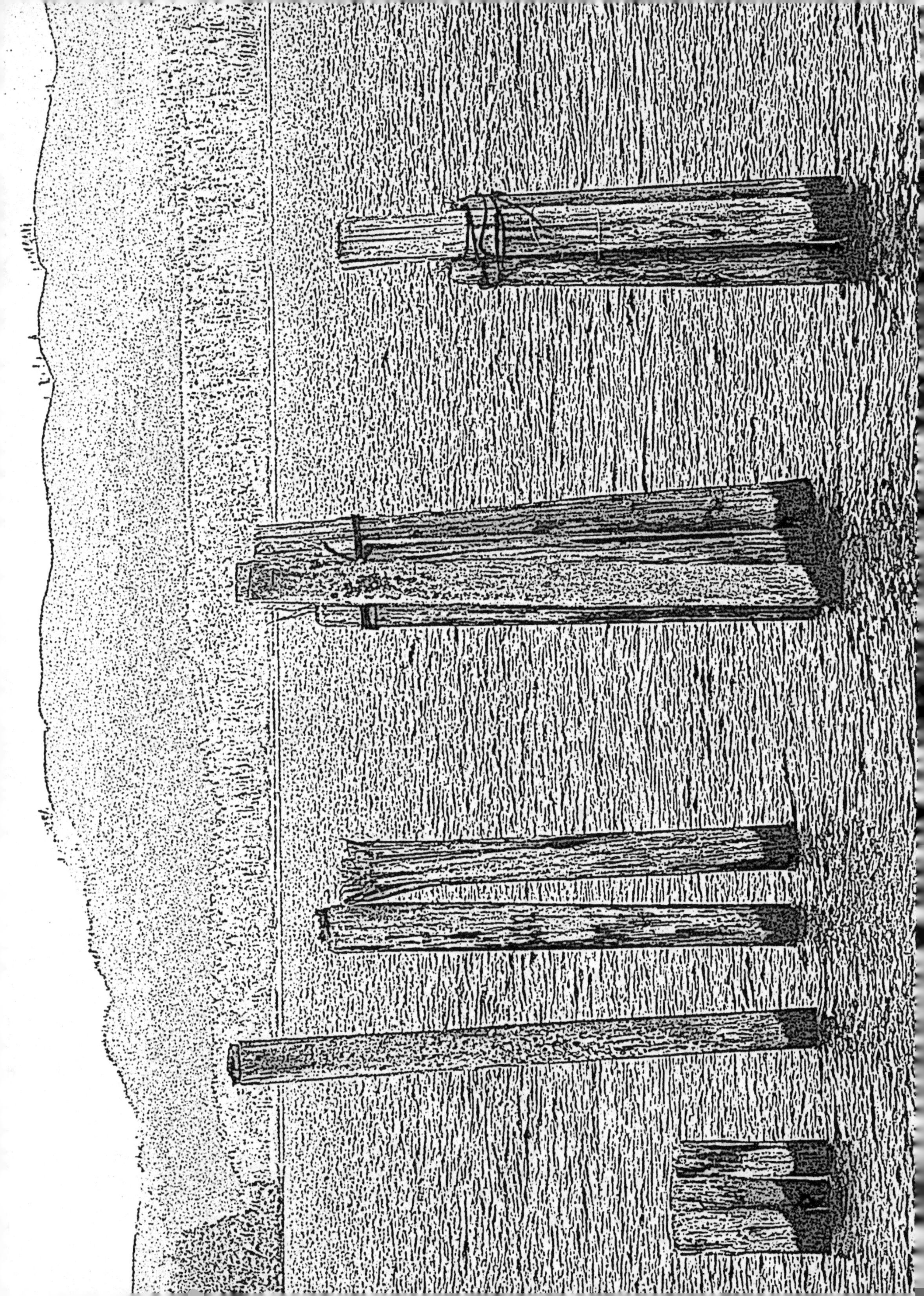

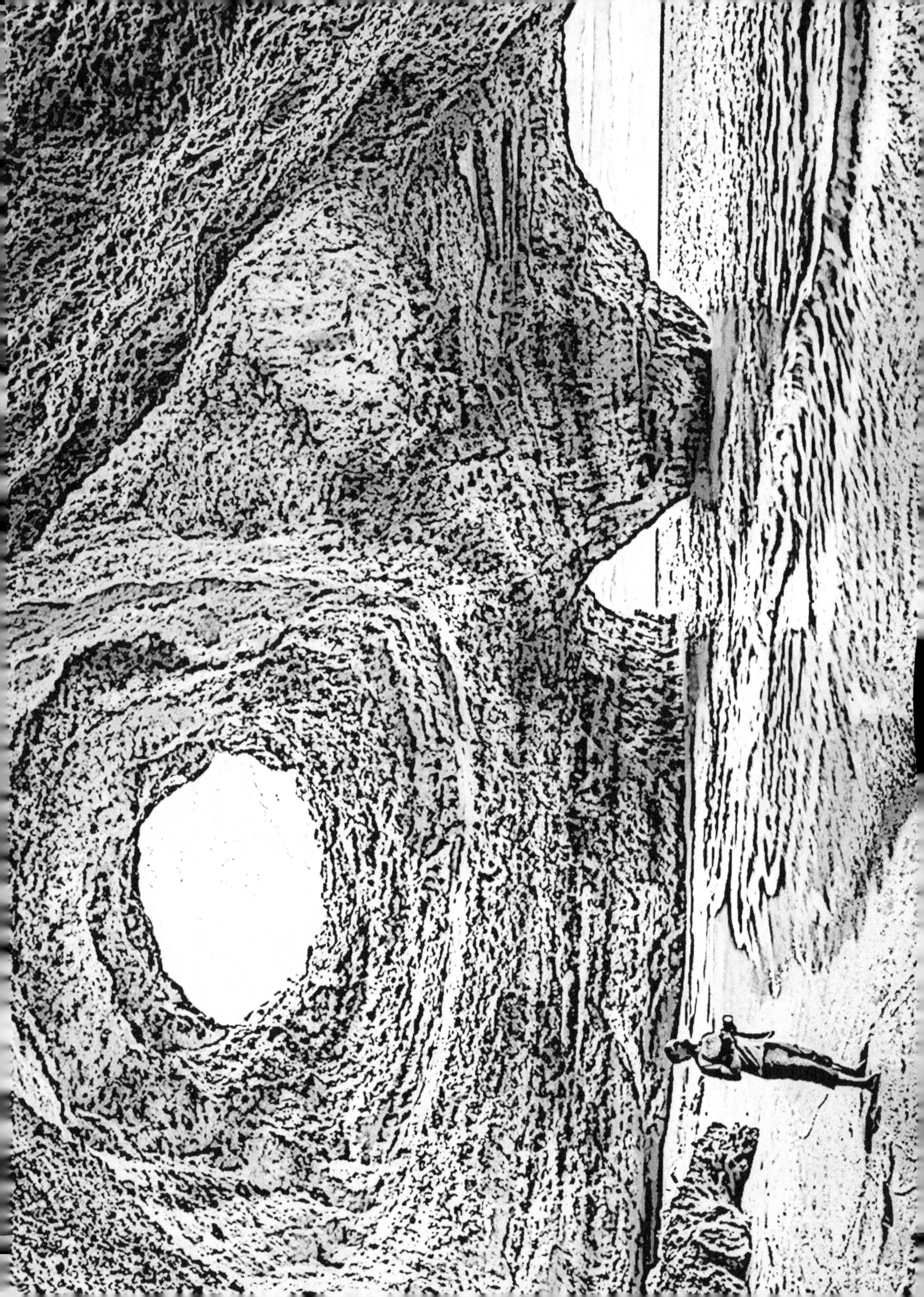

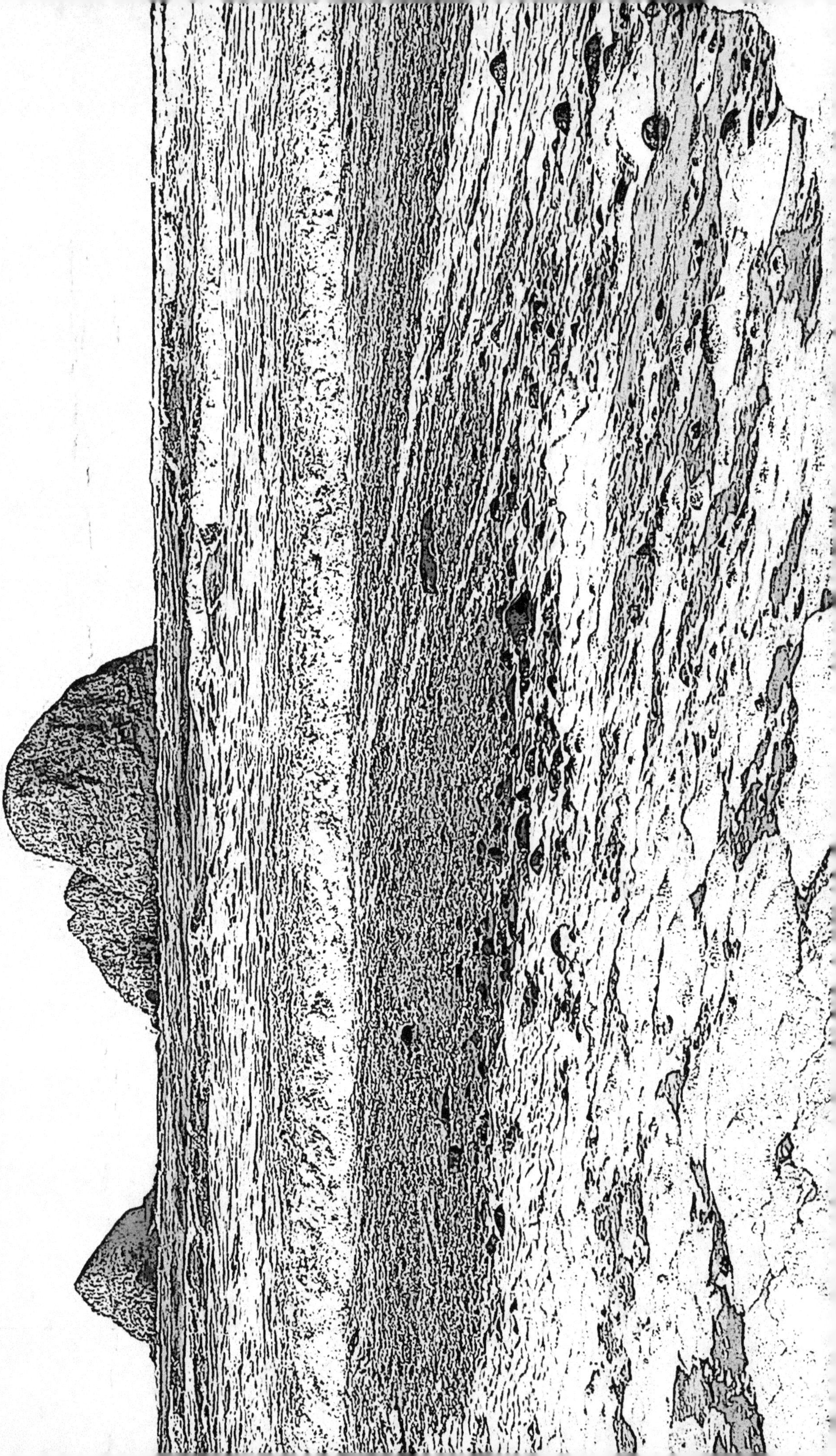

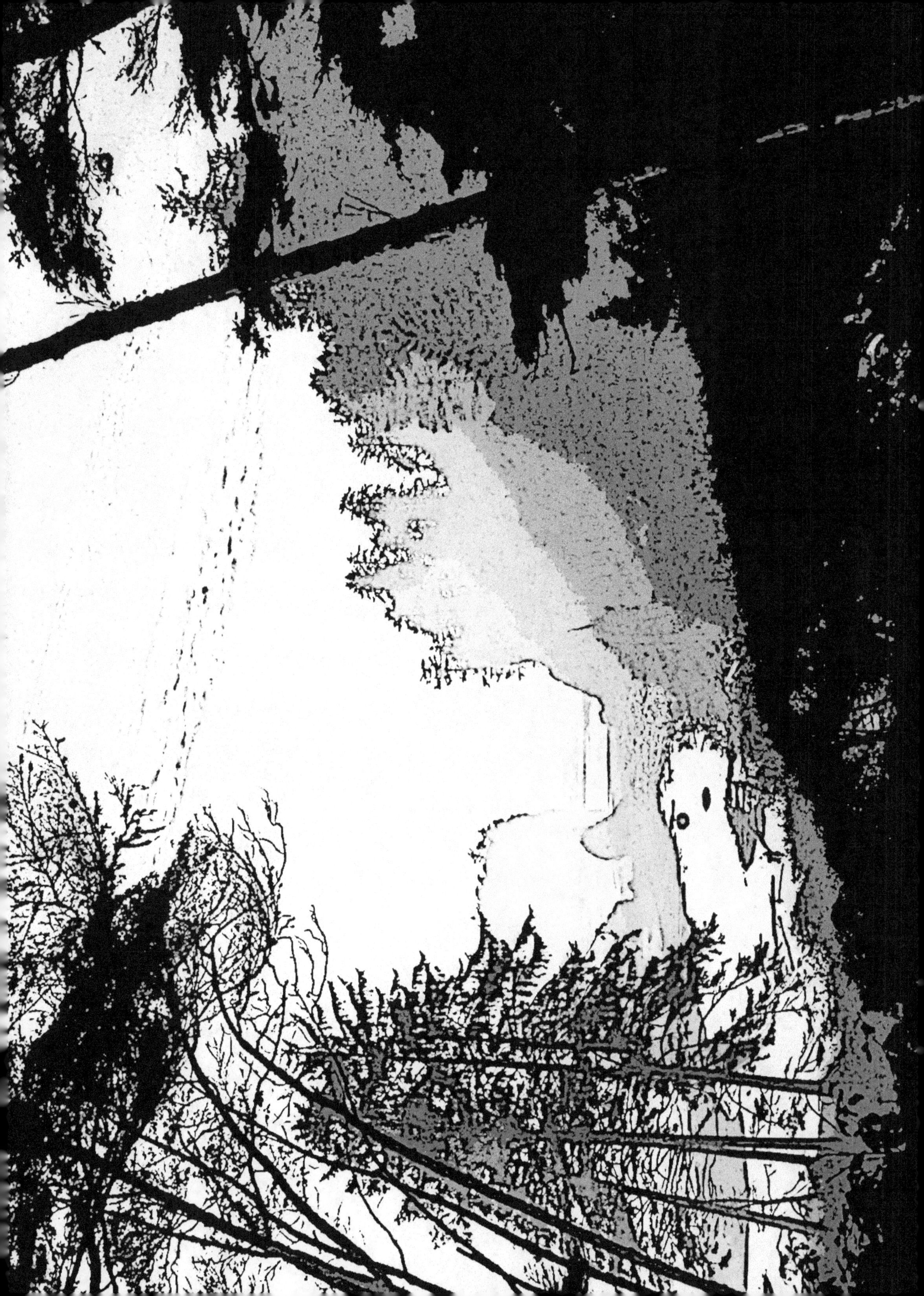

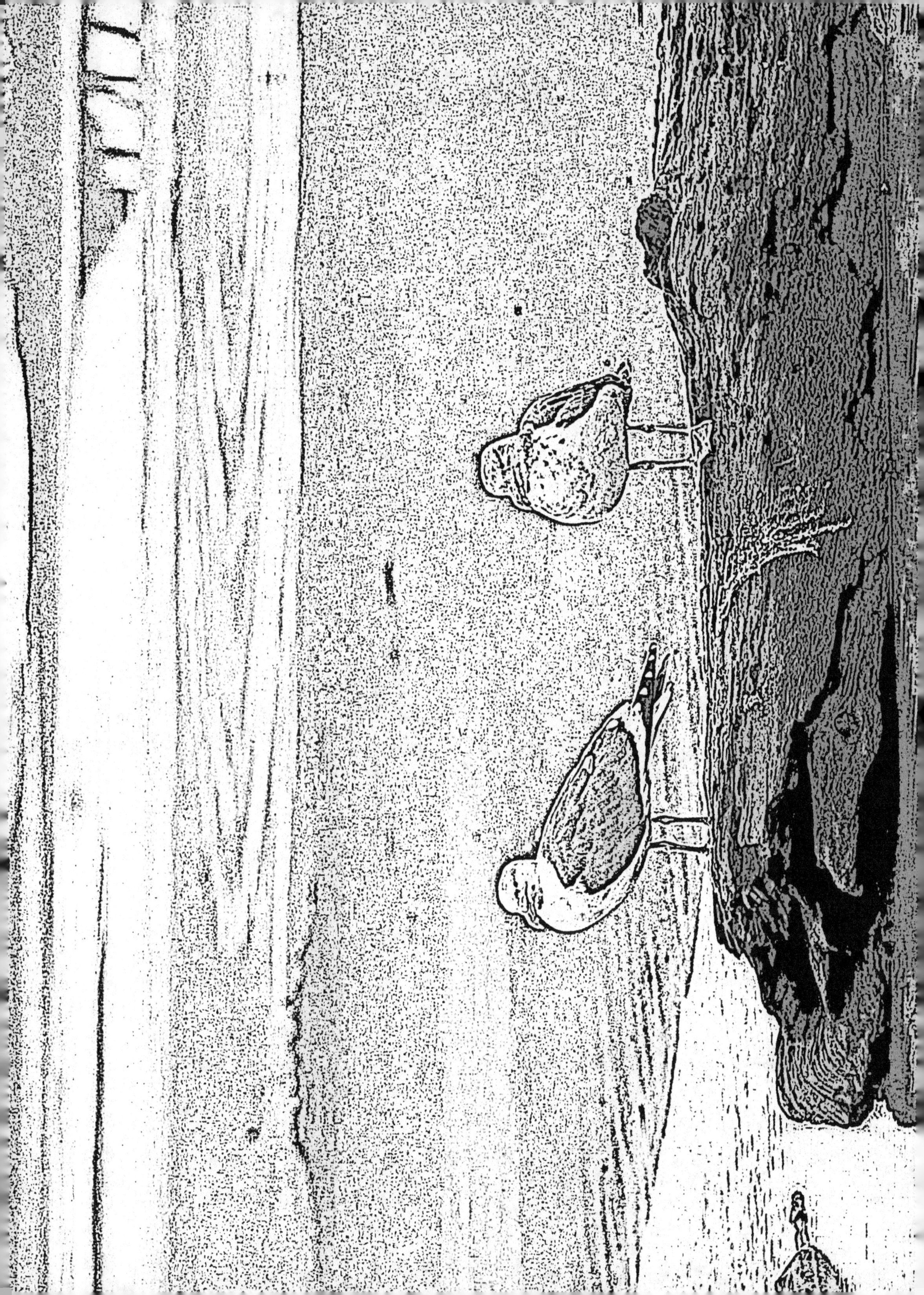

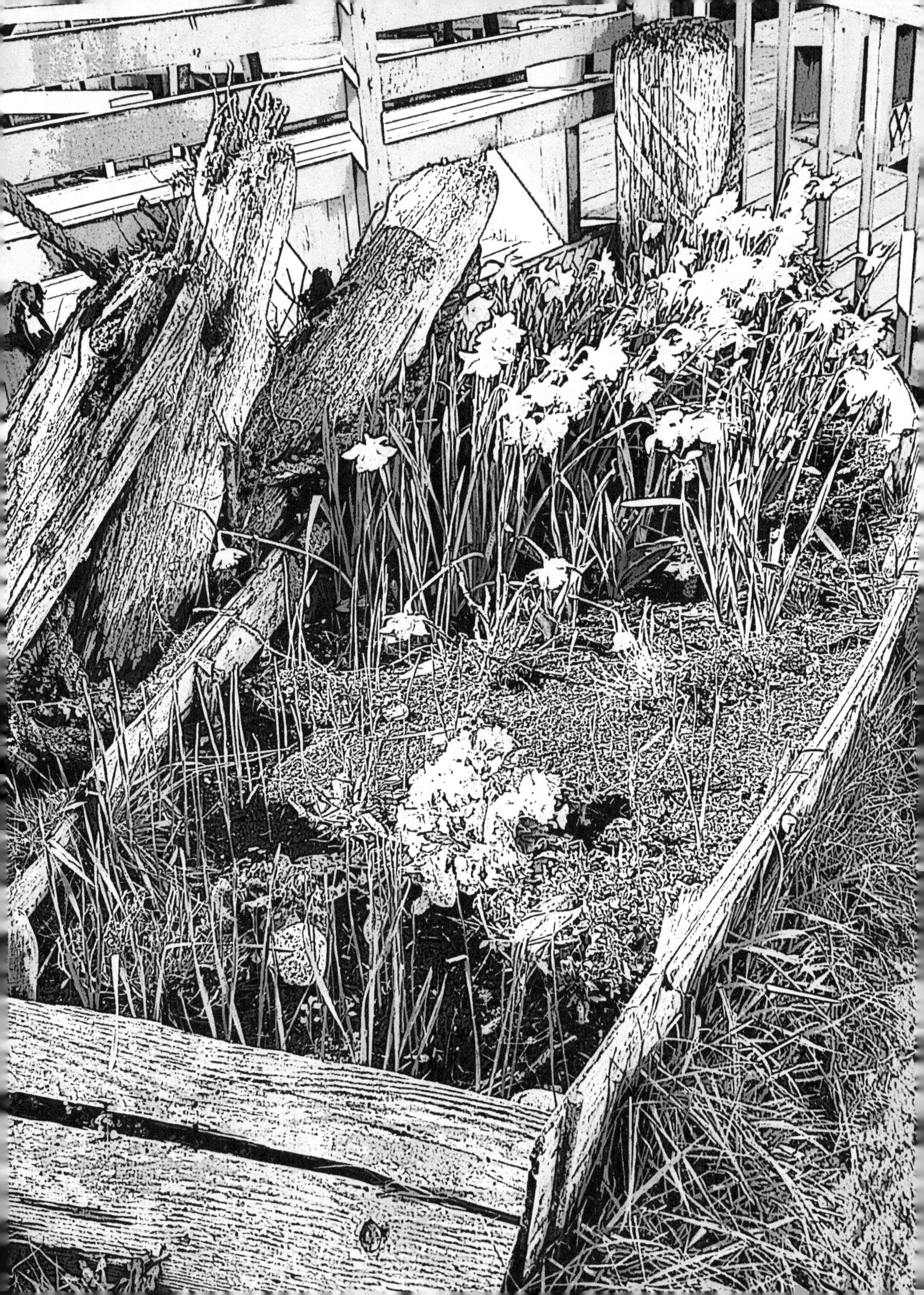

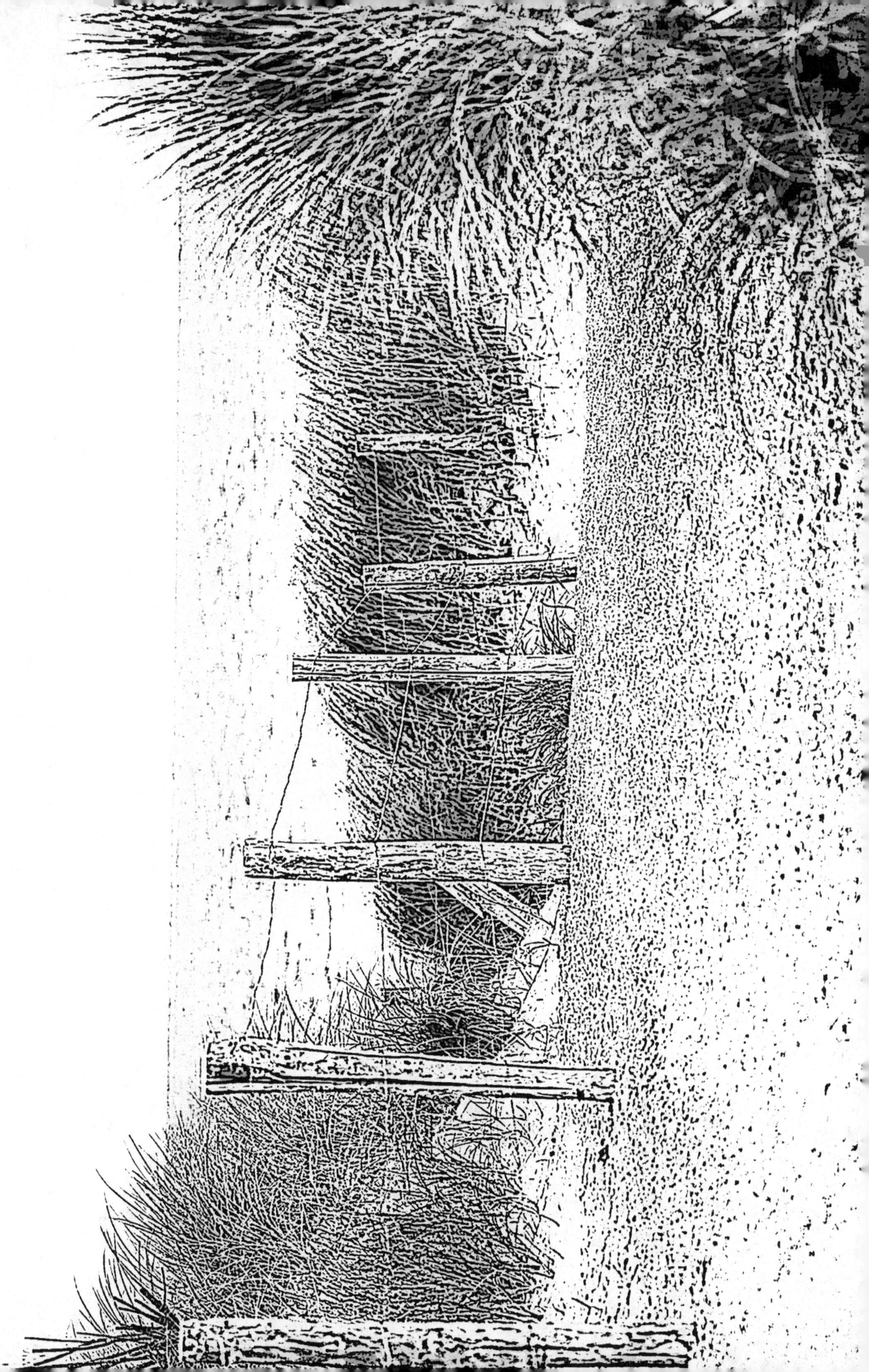

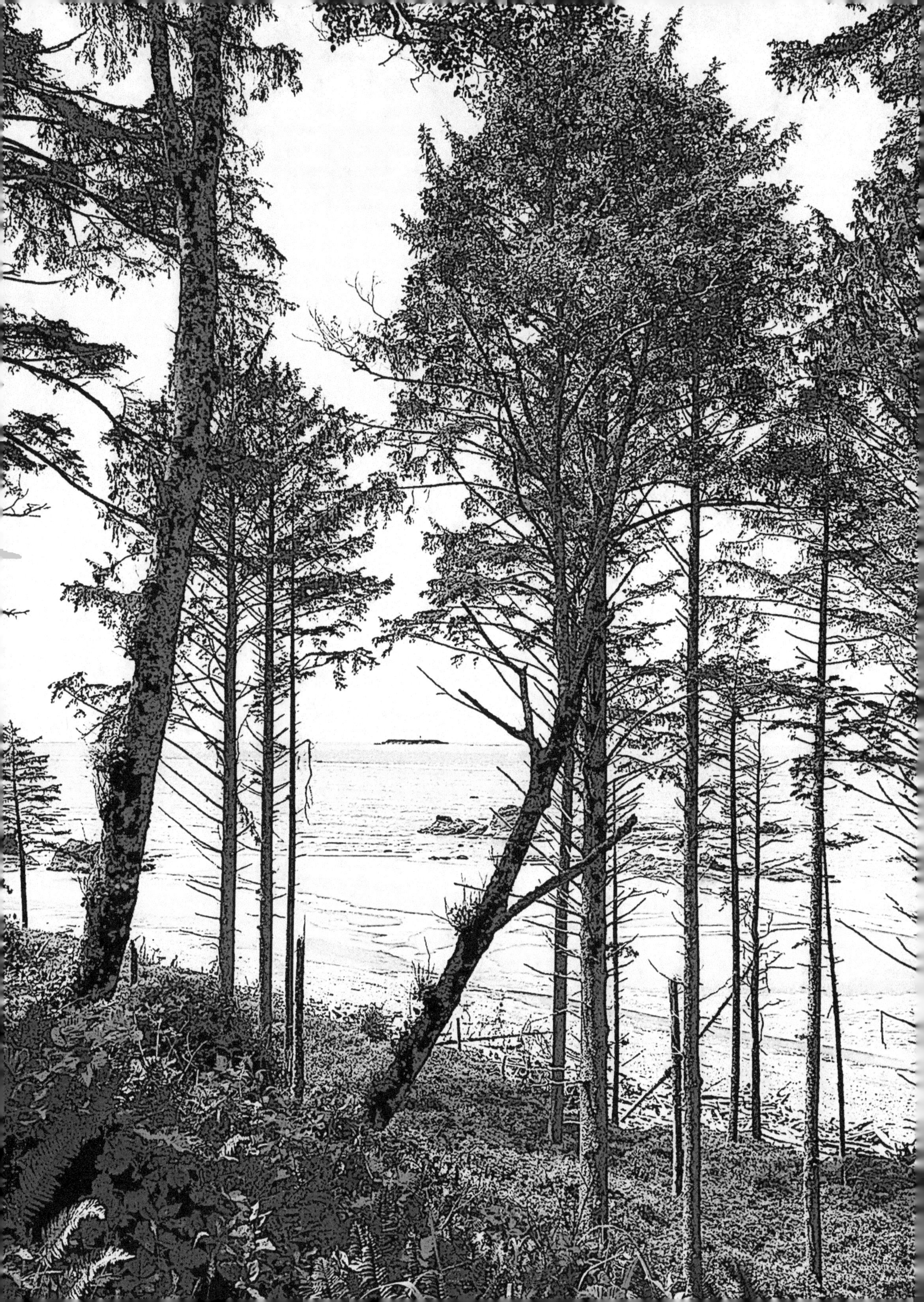

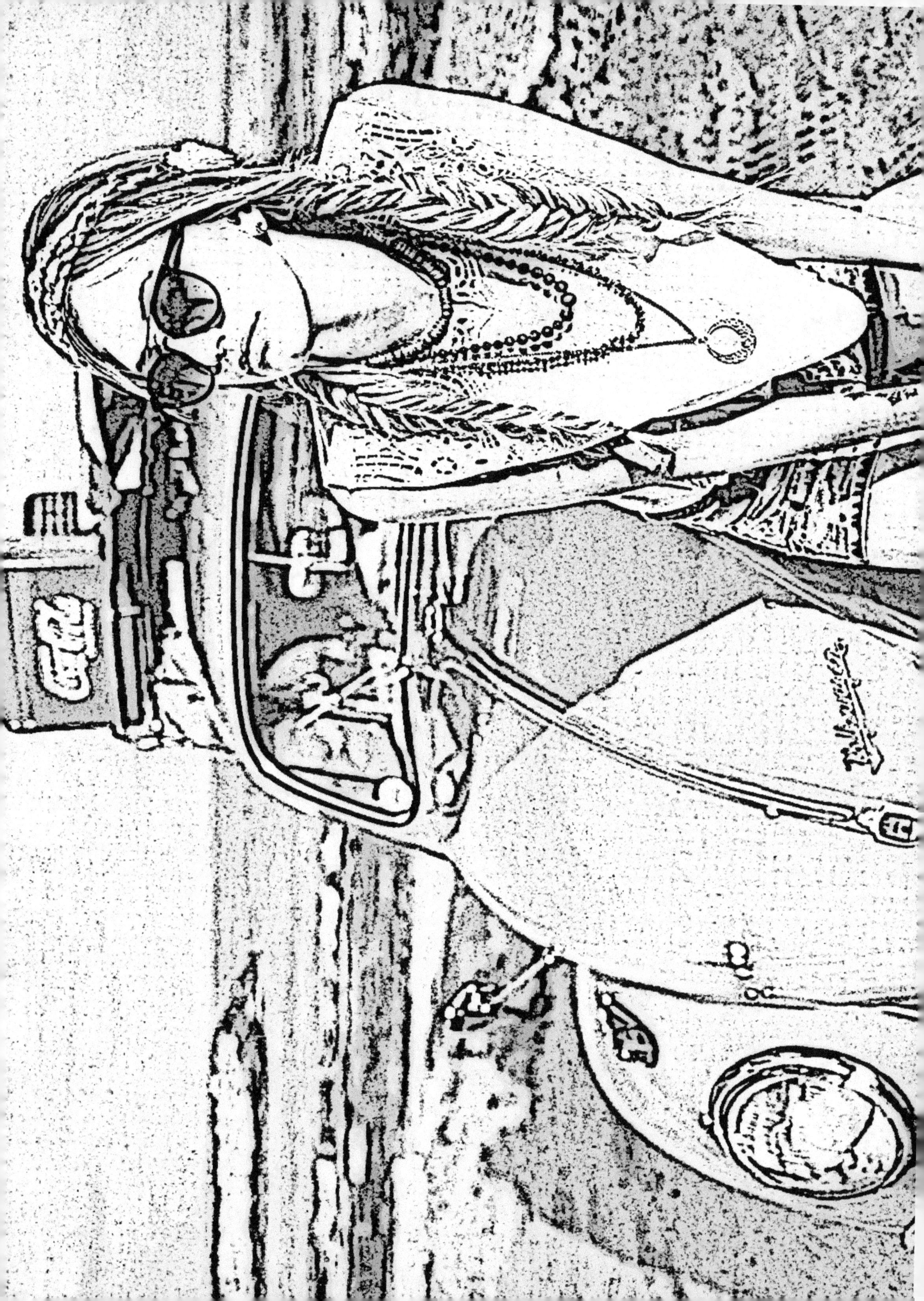

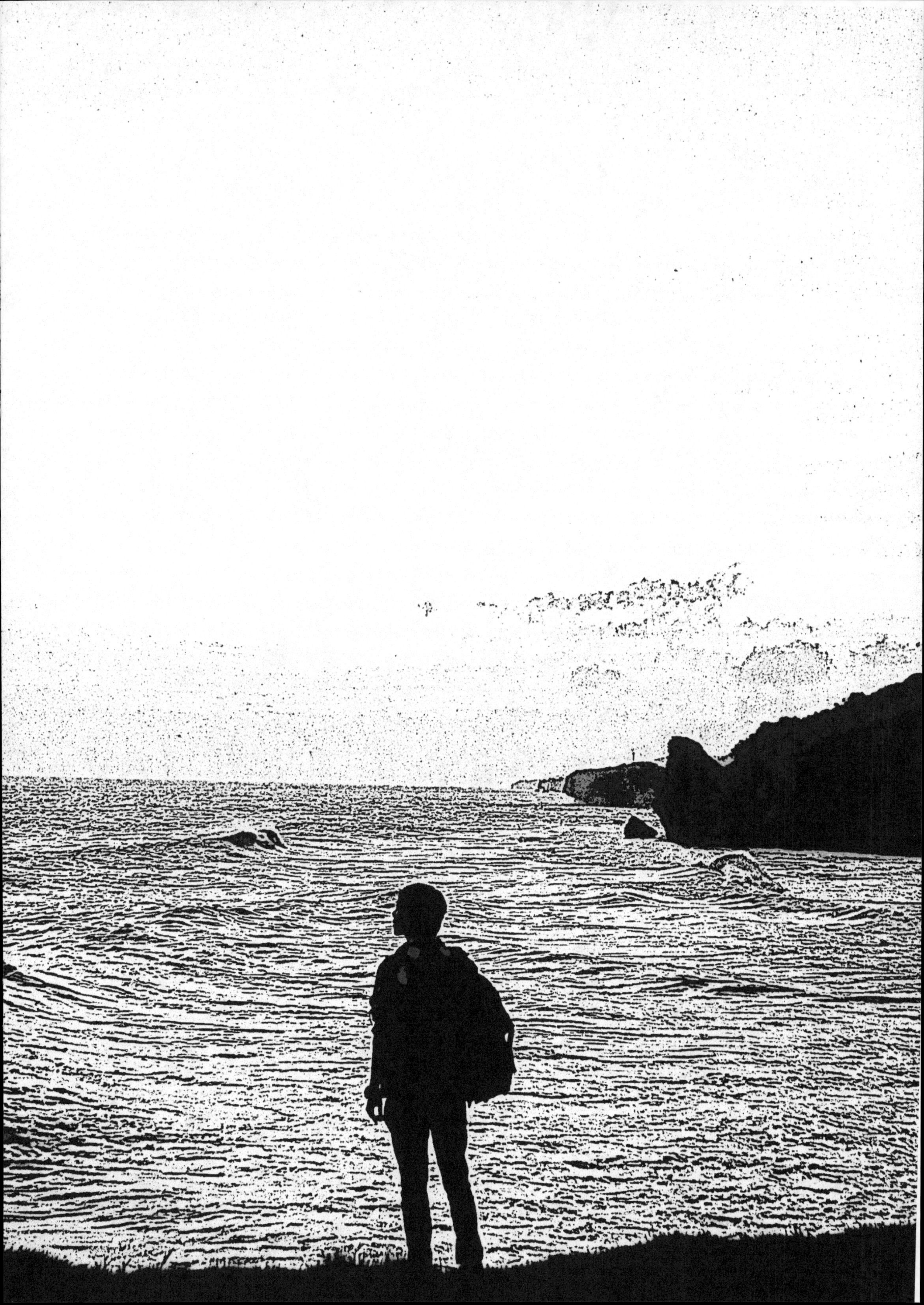

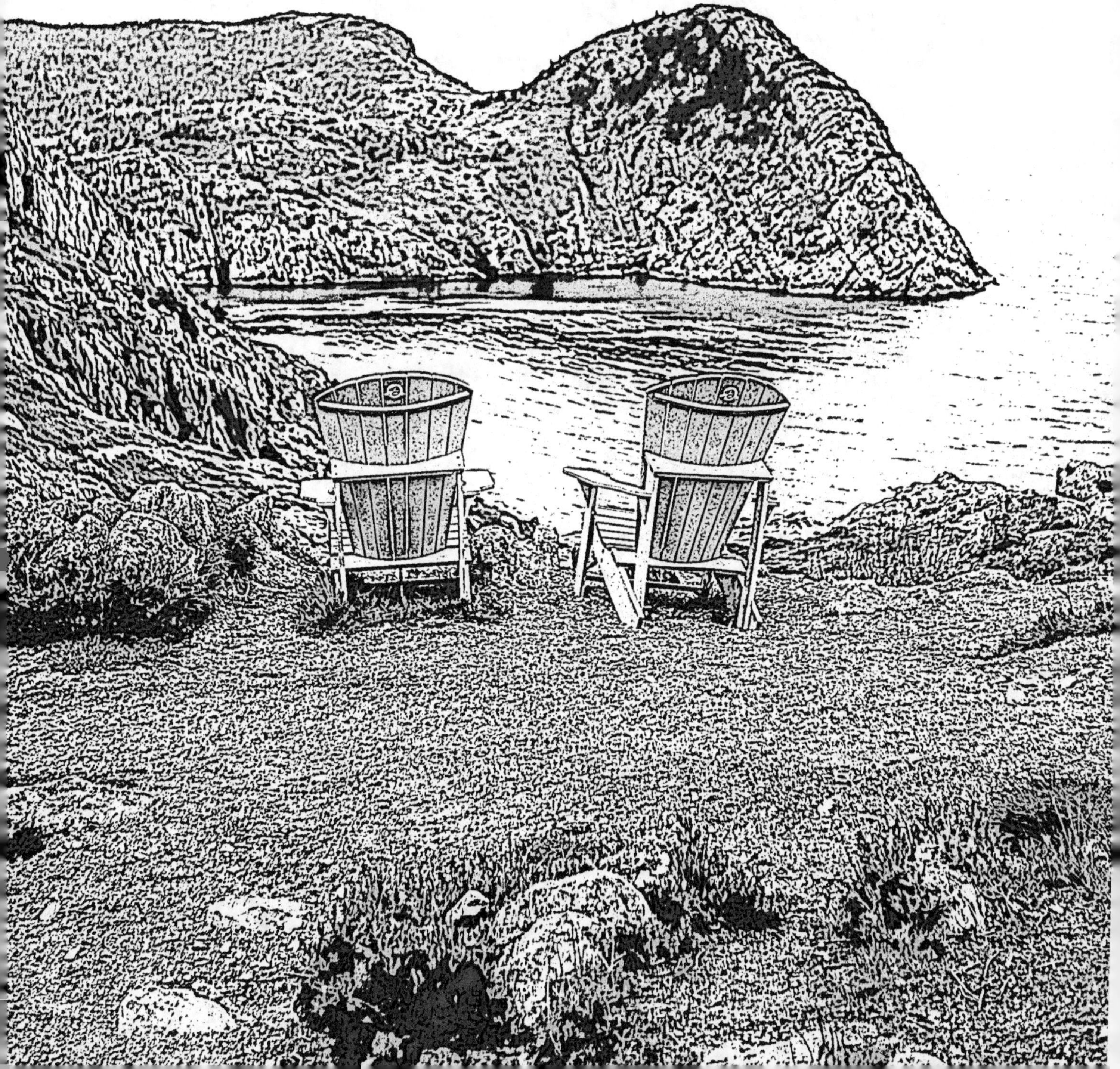

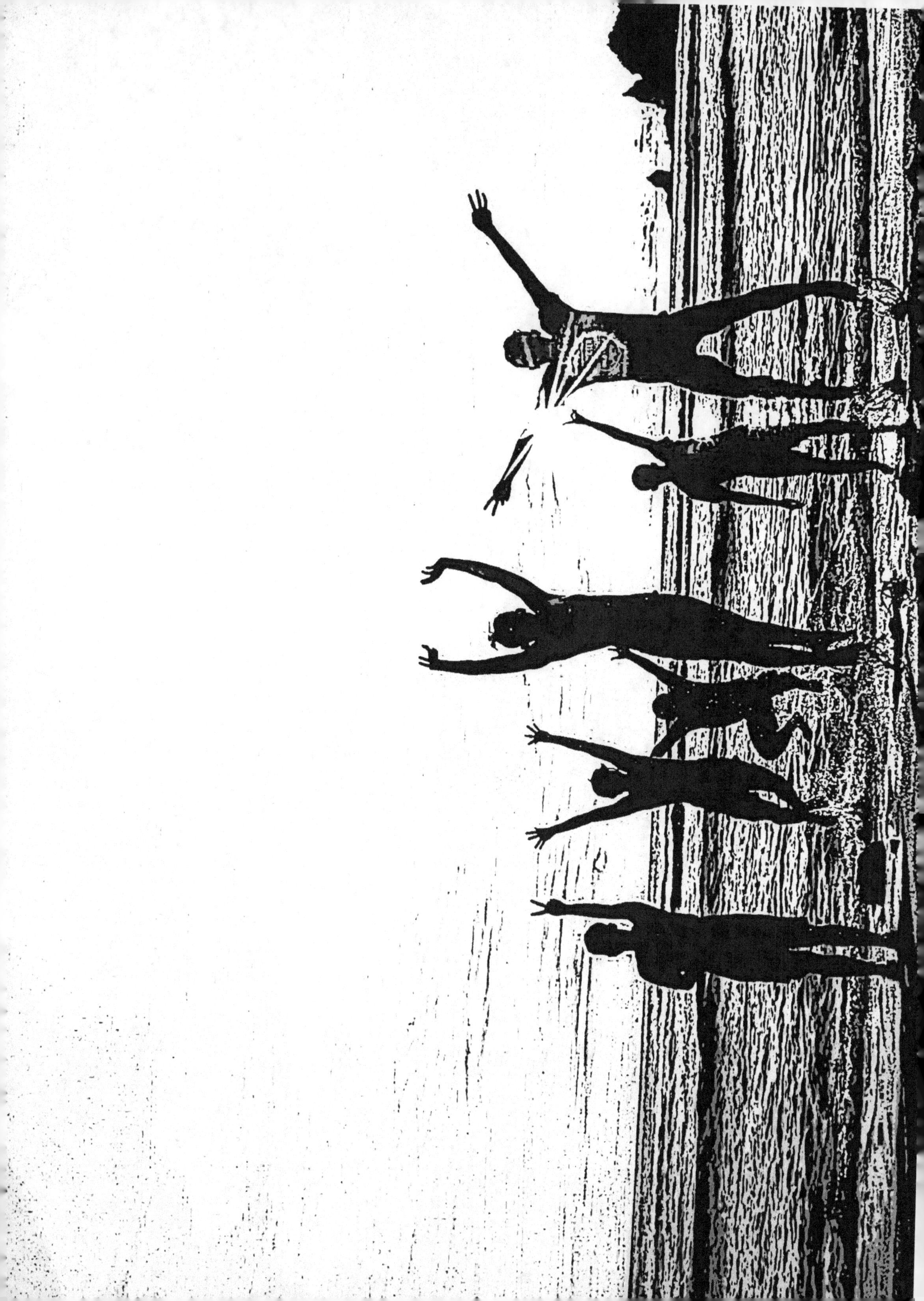

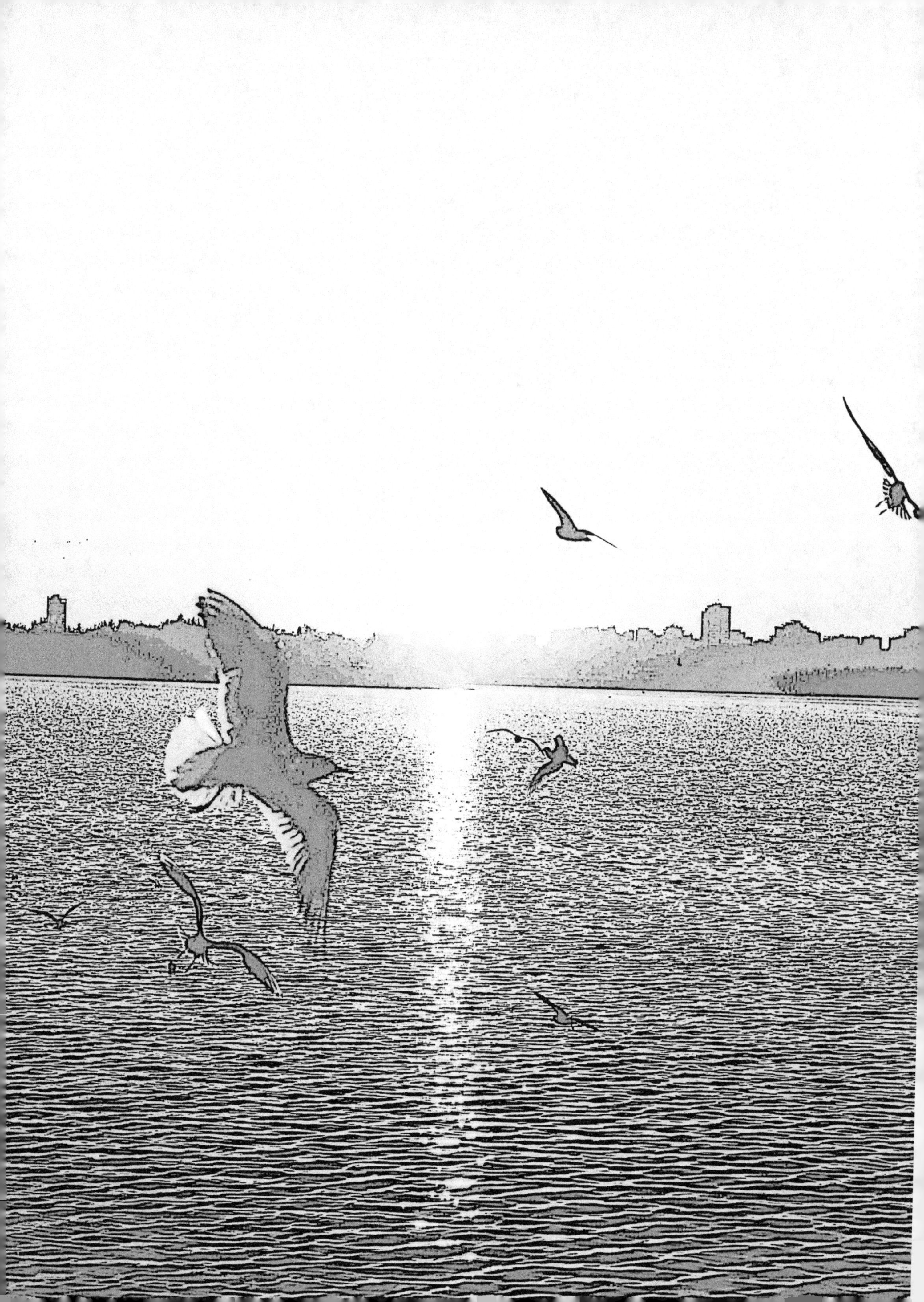

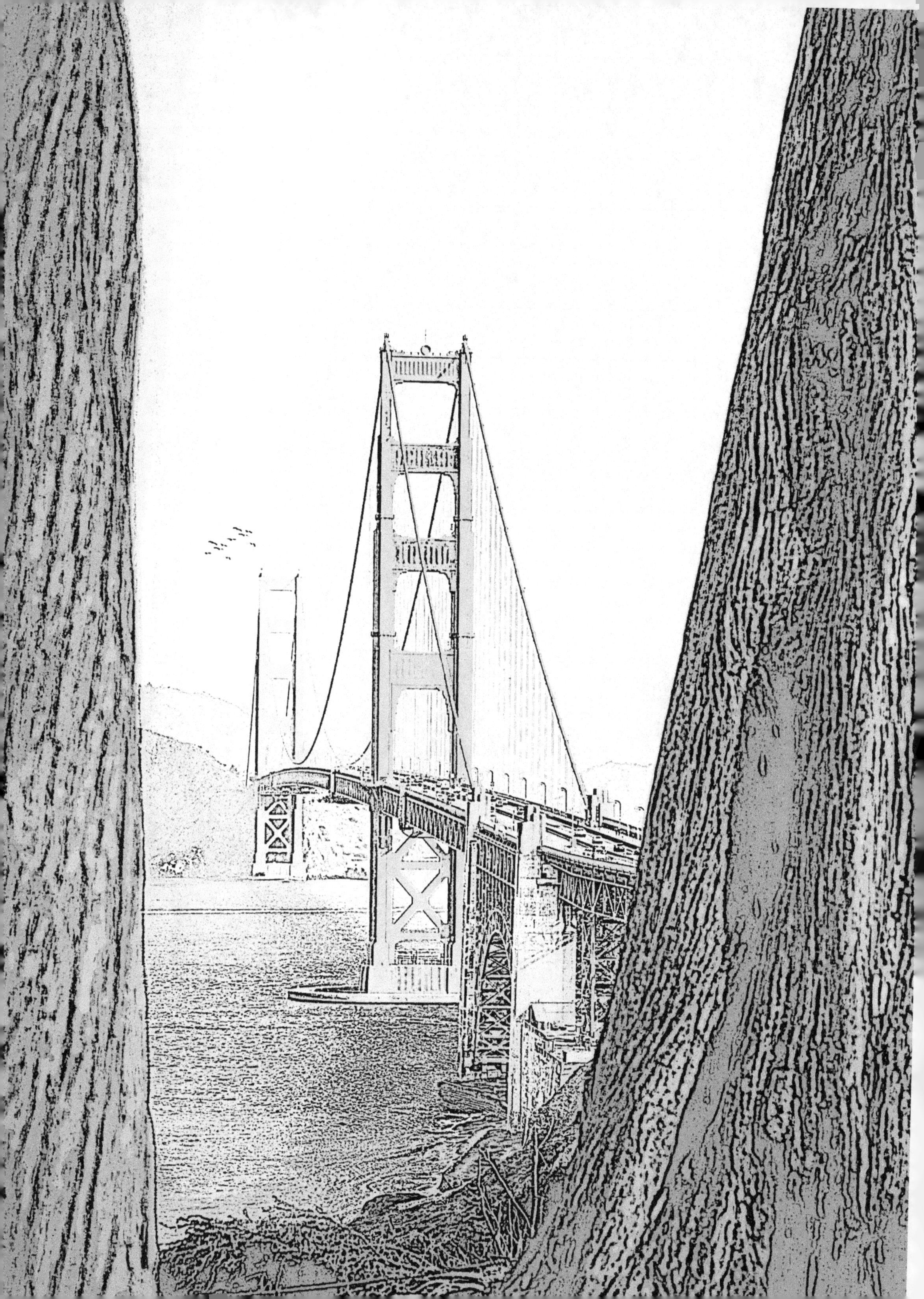

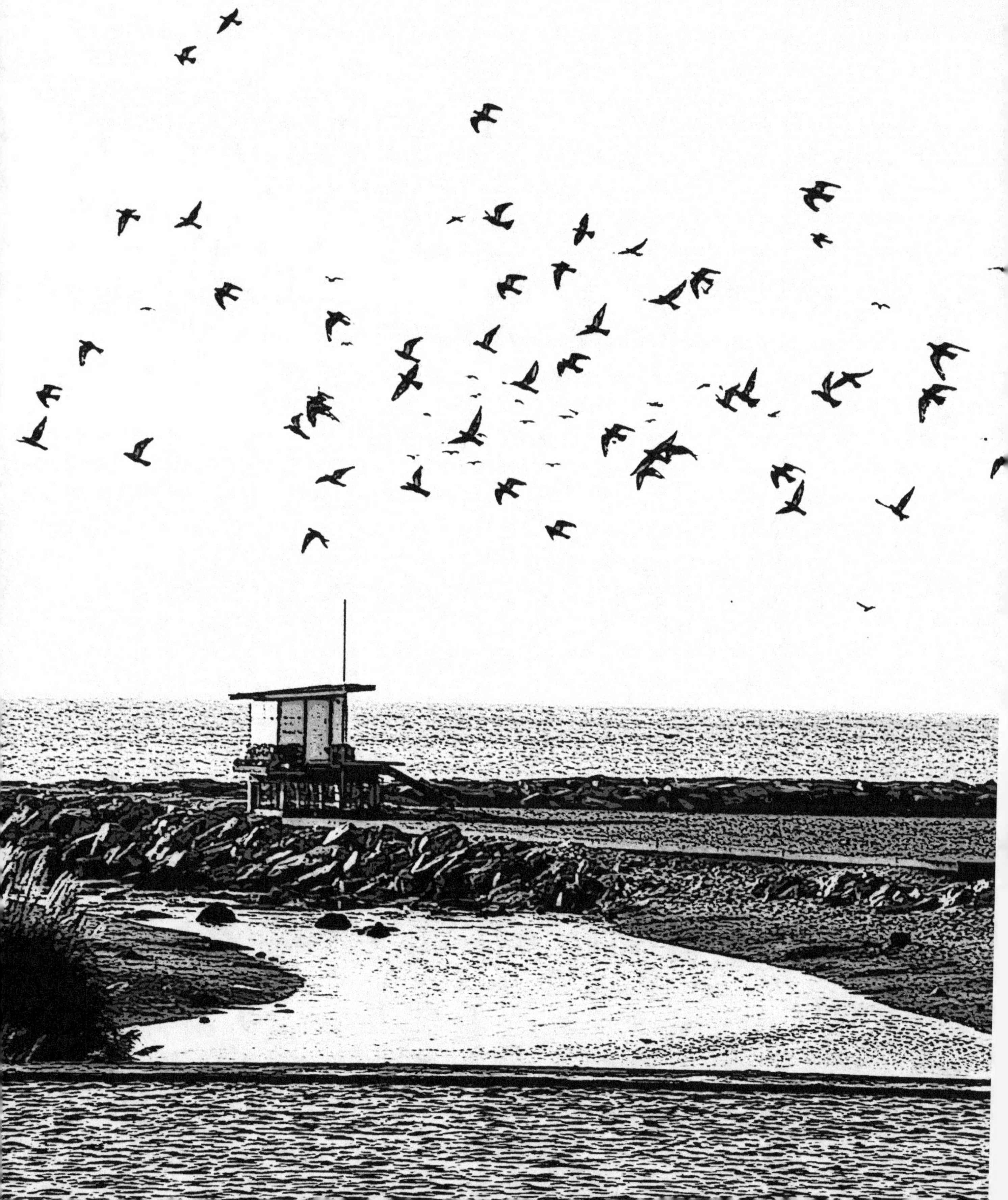

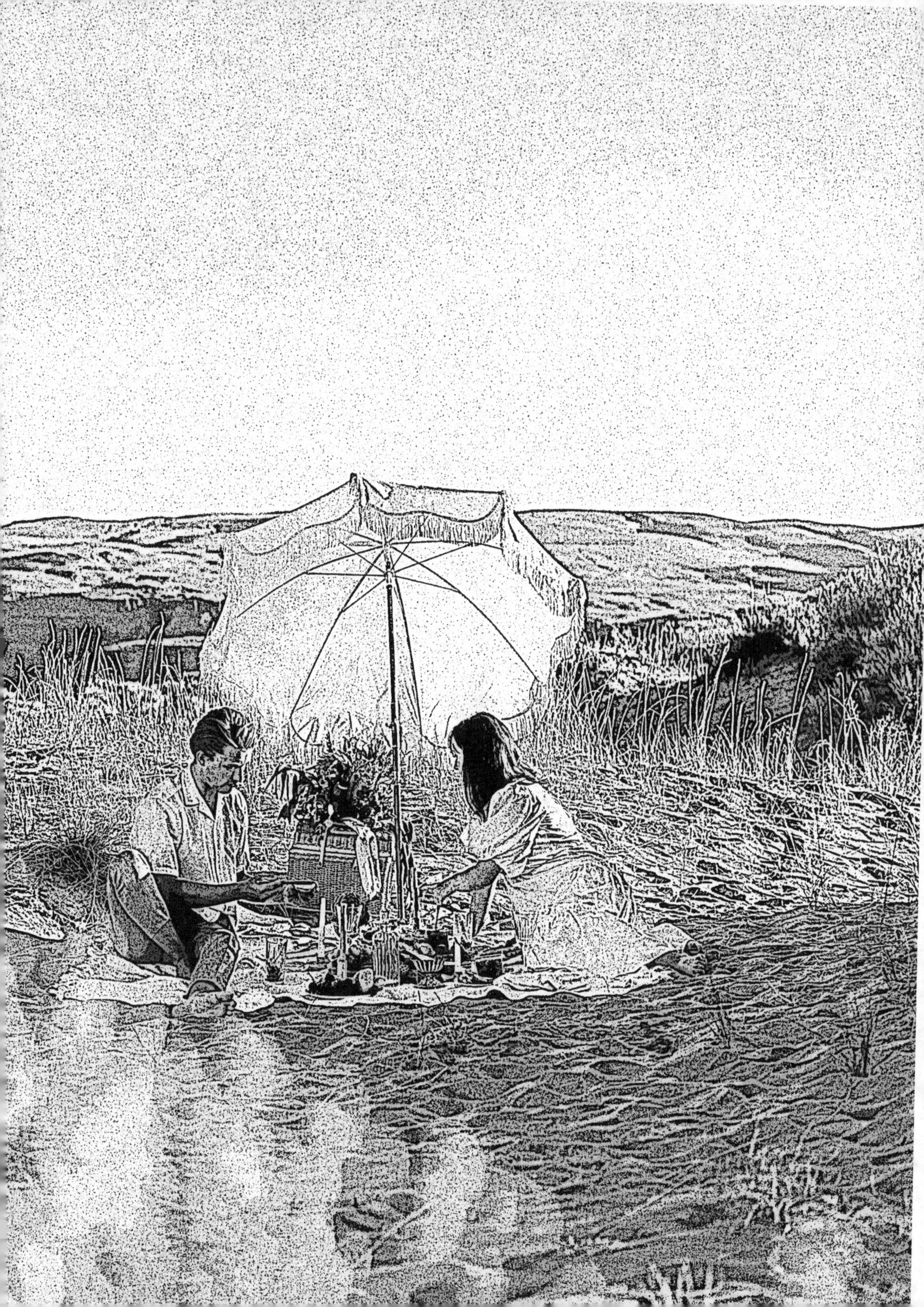

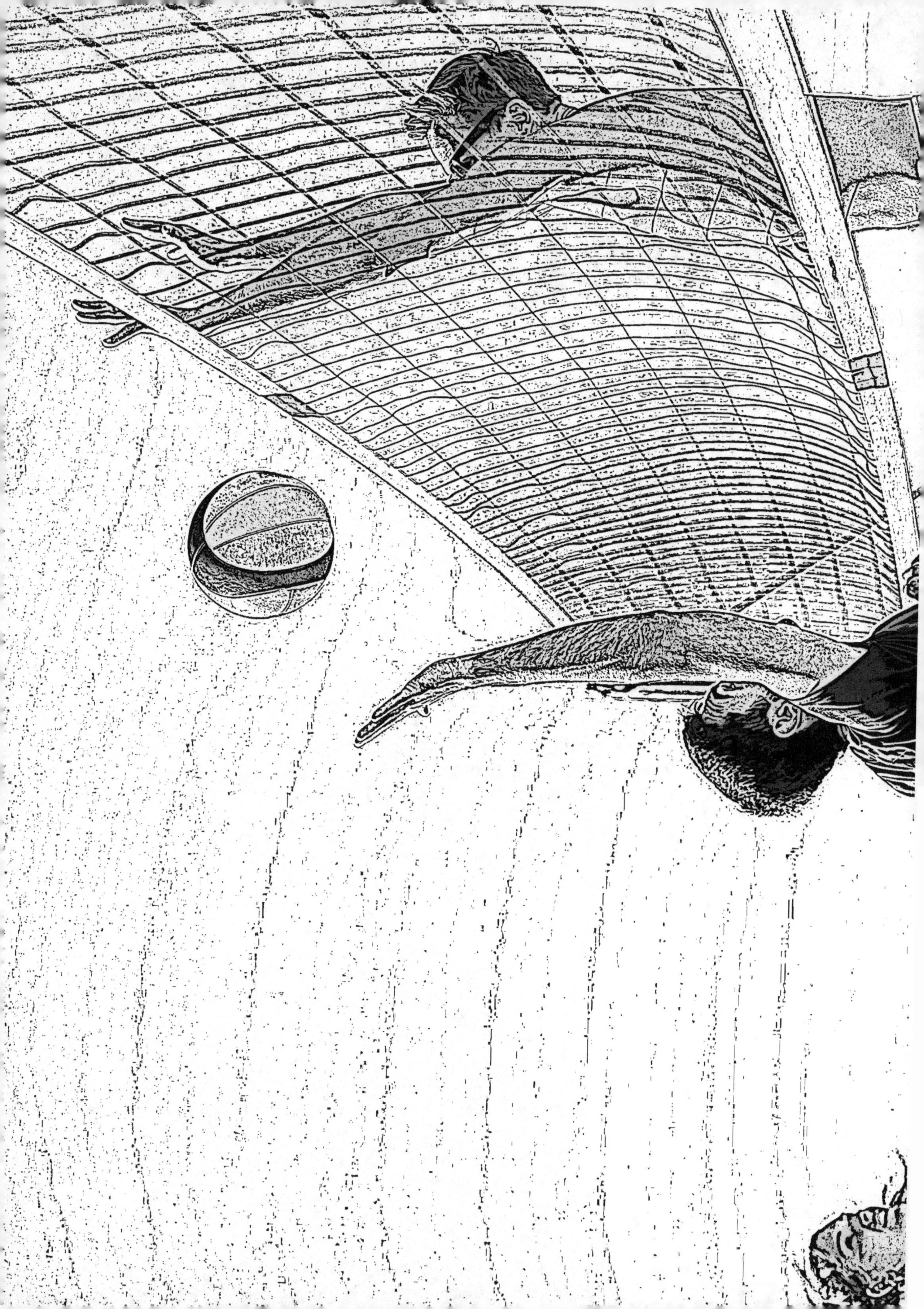

www.ingramcontent.com/pod-product-compliance
Lightning Source LLC
Chambersburg PA
CBHW080555220526
45466CB00010B/3158